Richard G. Beauchamp

Bichon Frise

Everything About Purchase, Care, Nutrition, Behavior, and Training

Filled with Full-color Photographs
Illustrations by Michele Earle-Bridges

BARRON'S

CONTENTS

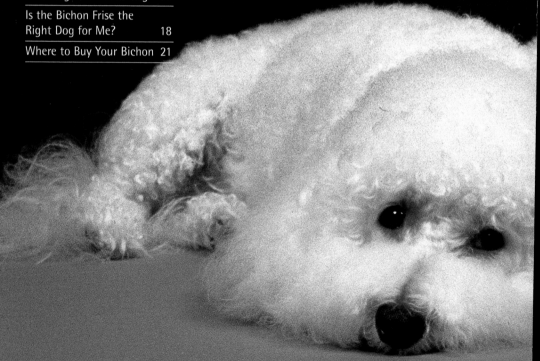

THE HISTORY AND ORIGIN OF THE BICHON FRISE

As difficult as it may be to imagine, the diminutive and delicate-looking Italian Greyhound, the stalwart Bulldog, the massive Great Dane and yes, even the little white tornado lying on your sofa, the Bichon Frise, can all be traced to a common ancestor. That ancestor is none other than the one we know today as **Canis lupus,** *the wolf.*

Origin

The wolf's transition from antagonist to "man's best friend" began somewhere in the Mesolithic period, which was more than ten thousand years ago. Just providing food for self and family and staying out of harm's way was undoubtedly the Mesolithic human's major concern in life. This in itself was no mean feat, considering that the use of tools was extremely limited at this stage of human development.

Observation of the wolf might have taught humans some effective hunting techniques to use themselves, also many of the wolf's social habits may well have seemed strikingly familiar. The association grew from there.

The Bichon Frise's entire history reveals how closely the breed has been associated with humans. Darlings of the royal courts, sea-faring companions, and street entertainers—all in the company of their owners.

As the relationship developed through the ages, certain descendants of these increasingly domesticated wolves could be advantageously selected to assist in hunting and other techniques of survival. Wolves that could assist in satisfying the unending human need for food were of course most highly prized.

Also valued were those wolves that made some kind of warning sound when a marauding neighbor or beast of prey threatened the settlement. Wolves that performed any function that aided early human existence were cherished and allowed to breed, whereas those that were not helpful or whose temperament proved incompatible were driven away.

With the passing of time humans realized they could manipulate breedings of these wolves-cum-dogs so that the resulting offspring were extremely proficient in particular areas. While human populations developed a more sophisticated lifestyle, they also thought up new ways in which these domesticated wolves could be of assistance. Customizing the evolving wolves to suit growing human needs was the next step. They became hunting wolves, guard wolves, and herding wolves. The list of useful duties grew and grew.

Romans Classify the Breeds

One can find documentation of controlled breeding practices by Roman writers as early as the first century A.D. The Romans had actually broken down the various types of dogs into six general classifications very similar to the "variety groups" used as a classification method by the American Kennel Club today. Two thousand years ago Roman writers talked of "house guardian dogs, shepherd dogs, sporting dogs, war dogs, scent dogs, and sight dogs."

Many of our modern breeds can trace their ancestry directly to members of these early groups. Combining two or more individuals from these different categories developed yet other breeds.

One of these combinations created a family of dogs known as the *barbichons* (later shortened to *bichons*). This new family was developed with the use of a medium- to large-size water dog called the Barbet and a family of generally white, small "lap" or ladies' dogs that existed around the Mediterranean. These little white dogs traced as far back as 600–300 B.C. Several breeds of dogs are known to have descended from this origin, including the Toy Poodle, the Maltese, and four "varieties" or subgroups of the Bichon family.

Because most wolves and wild dogs were rather large and dark in color, small, light-colored dogs were intriguing and admired. Thus the small white dogs became very popular and soon became members of the immediate household.

Often these companion dogs traveled with their owners. As trading flourished, the little pet dogs from home could be bartered for something else wanted or needed. The little "bichons" that had eventually evolved accompanied their owners to different parts of the world and were left there as trade for other goods. The dogs soon became established and flourished, developing into four distinct varieties: the Bichon Maltaise, the Bichon Bolognaise, the Bichon Havanese (also known as the Havana Silk Dog), and the Bichon Tenerife. The Bichon Tenerife was to become today's Bichon Frise.

The Four Bichon Varieties

No one is positive about what other canine mixtures may have been involved at the various places to which these four varieties of Bichon immigrated. There does seem to be agreement that the first of the group, the Bichon Maltaise, flourished on the isle of Malta.

Whether this breed is the ancestor of today's Maltese remains controversial. Those who subscribe to this theory offer as proof the recurring and highly undesirable woolly coat that some Maltese have. The Maltese coat must be straight and silky, with no undercoat whatsoever.

Another branch of the family, the Bolognaise, became popular around the Italian city of Bologna. They could often be seen accompanying members of the royal family and members of the court. History records that Bolognaise were often sent as gifts to members of the French and Spanish royal households as well.

There is scant anatomical difference between today's Bichon Bolognaise and the Bichon Frise (originally the Tenerife). Primarily, the Bolognaise temperament is less outgoing than that of its cousin, and the Bolognaise is presented in the show ring with scissoring done only around the eyes and feet.

Other migrations of these little dogs began in the eastern Mediterranean and disembarked in Spain. They eventually found their way along the trade routes to Cuba. It appears the Spanish sailors took the little dogs with them, and the ones remaining in Cuba are credited as the forebears of the Bichon variety known as the Havanese.

The Havanese is the smaller member of the four cousins, normally measuring about 8 to 11 inches (20–28 cm) at the shoulder. It is much shorter in leg, longer in body, and comes in a wide variety of colors.

It seems highly probable that these same Spanish sailors took other members of the Bichon family with them in their trading expeditions to the Canary Islands and Tenerife. How long these Bichons remained there and what other blood entered the gene pool is unknown, but the Bichon seems to have flourished in the Canary Islands and Tenerife as well. Eventually their descendants made their way full circle, not only back to Spain but to Italy as well. This variety of Bichon was known as the Bichon Tenerife, and the breed carried that name for many years.

The Bichon Frise Gets Its Name

So, then, where did our little white dog we now know as the Bichon Frise actually come from? There are conflicting answers, but *The Encyclopedia of Dogs* (Thomas Y. Cromwell Co., New York), which was produced with the cooperation and direction of the Federation Cynologique Internationale (F.C.I.), gives the

The Bichon Frise's early ancestors often traveled the world as companions to their seafaring owners.

actual country of origin as France. The F.C.I. is the august organization that presides over all of Europe's canine activities, so if anyone has the answers on European dogs, it should be the F.C.I.

History substantiates a series of French invasions of Italy that lasted through most of the 1500s. During that time the French came under the Renaissance influence and adopted Italian culture. Part of the adoption process included the Bichon Tenerife, which then made its appearance in France under Francis I, the patron of the Renaissance, who reigned from 1515 to 1547.

From that point it seems the breed went undercover for a time, but it emerged again briefly as a favorite of the court during the reign of Napoleon III in the early 1800s. By the end of that same century, however, the popularity of the darling of the courtesans had diminished again. The Bichon Tenerife became the common dog running the streets, but the breed's agility and ability to learn quickly provided a new direction and preserved the breed from extinction.

Even then it was not at all unusual to find the Bichon that could jump many times its own height, walk on its hind legs for long distances, and do somersaults. These same capabilities exist in many strains of the breed today.

Organ grinders and peddlers were quick to put the Bichon's crowd-pleasing antics to use, and soon the little dogs began performing tricks on street corners and in the circuses and fairs throughout France. The little Bichons clowned about, pawing the air as though begging for money and applause, and their owners reaped the monetary rewards. The breed's characteristic of pawing the air was of course highly prized by

The Bichon's powder puff appearance belies the fact that the breed is a determined and sturdy little dog. The breed managed to survive the rigors of two World Wars and the fads and fashions of centuries.

the organ grinders and evidently selected for in breeding programs, as it has become an established trait of the breed.

World War I nearly cost the Bichon its life as a breed, but for its incredible hardiness and will to survive. Soldiers of many countries, enchanted by the sturdy and clever white charmers, departed for home with Bichons as pets. But none of these isolated specimens appears to have been used to initiate a breeding program.

Finally, with decimated stock somewhat replenished by interested breeders after World War I, the first official standard of excellence was written for the Bichon Tenerife in France and adopted by the Societé Centrale Canine in March 1933. This standard gave the breed its first official and far more descriptive name, the Bichon à Poil Frise (the Bichon of the Curly Hair), more popularly referred to as the Bichon Frise.

With the advent of yet another war in Europe the newly named Bichon had to withstand another devastating blow to its numbers. Again the tenacity of the breed and of those devoted to the breed prevailed, and the Bichon somehow managed to survive. Fortunately the early 1950s proved a turning point for the breed when it embarked upon a journey to America.

The Bichon Comes to America

Helene and François Picault of Dieppe, France, had become interested in the Bichon Frise and began to breed and also show their dogs at various all-breed events. The Picaults migrated to Milwaukee, Wisconsin, in 1952, bringing with them their rapidly growing family of Bichons in hopes of popularizing and selling the breed in the United States.

Helen and François Picault of Dieppe, France brought the first Bichon Frise show-quality dogs to America.

Unfortunately their enthusiasm and hopes for the breed in America met with little response or success. Neither did the Picaults appreciate Milwaukee's frigid winters. They decided to move, taking their dogs with them to Southern California, where they came in contact with Collie breeder Gertrude Fournier. Mrs. Fournier became enchanted with the breed and struggled valiantly to achieve popularity for it in the United States, but it was not until she enlisted the interest and support of Barbara Stubbs of La Jolla, California, that a successful plan was initiated and followed. A club devoted to promoting the best interests of the breed was organized under the name Bichon Frise Club of America, and serious efforts began to make it better known.

The Breed Catches On

In the late 1960s, with the promotional assistance of *Kennel Review* magazine, owned by the author, the breed caught the attention of U.S. dog show exhibitors. Within just a few years the Bichon Frise skyrocketed to popularity with those who were breeding and showing dogs under American Kennel Club jurisdiction. By this time the breed had become popularly referred to as simply the Bichon.

In April 1973 the Bichon Frise was recognized by the American Kennel Club (AKC) and admitted to compete for championship points as a member of the Non Sporting Group classification. In July of that same year the first all-breed Best in Show to be won by a Bichon Frise was awarded at Framington Valley Kennel Club. The dog was Phyllis Tabler's Champion Chaminade Syncopation. Syncopation was bred by Barbara Stubbs and the author.

Many more Best in Show awards were to follow for Syncopation and others of the breed. International popularity came rapidly for the

Bichon breed that was doing so well in the United States, and many American-bred Bichons were exported to all parts of the world.

In 1985 a female, Champion Devon Puff and Stuff, bred and owned by Nancy Shapland, was not only the top winner in her breed but also the top winner in the entire U.S. Non Sporting Group. Puff was a ringside favorite because of her antics in the show ring, often escaping from her handler and leading him on a merry chase.

On February 14, 2001, Ch. Special Times Just Right (call name J. R.) owned by Cecelia Ruggles, Eleanor McDonald, and Flavio Werneck, captured the ultimate award for purebred dogs by winning Best in Show at the famed Westminster Kennel Club dog show at Madison Square Garden in New York. The judge was Dorothy M. Macdonald, and Scott Sommer handled J. R. to the history-making win. The win was televised internationally, and J. R.'s charismatic personality captured the attention of dog lovers everywhere. AKC registrations for the breed have steadily increased with each passing year since that momentous event.

The Bichon Frise went from "new kid on the block" in 1973 to Best in Show at the prestigious Westminster Kennel Club in just over 25 years—a feat accomplished by few breeds even after centuries of recognition. The Bichon has captured a permanent place in the hearts of those who love dogs around the world.

Official AKC Standard for the Bichon Frise

The American Kennel Club, which is the chief registering agency for purebred dogs in America, provides a standard of excellence for every breed it recognizes. The standard stipulates all characteristics that an ideal specimen of the breed should have.

It must be remembered that no dog is perfect and that none adheres entirely to a given breed standard. The standard is used as a guideline by the breeder and as a blueprint by the dog judge to evaluate all entries.

General Appearance

The Bichon Frise is a small, sturdy, white powder puff of a dog whose merry temperament is evidenced by his plumed tail carried jauntily over the back and his dark-eyed inquisitive expression.

This is a breed that has no gross or incapacitating exaggerations and therefore there is no inherent reason for lack of balance or unsound movement.

Any deviation from the ideal described in the standard should be penalized to the extent of the deviation. Structural faults common to all breeds are as undesirable in the Bichon Frise as in any other breed, even though such faults may not be specifically mentioned in the standard.

Size, Proportion, Substance

Size—Dogs and bitches 9.5 to 11.5 inches [24.36–29.4 cm] are to be given primary preference. Only where the comparative superiority of a specimen outside this range clearly justifies it should greater latitude be taken. In no case, however, should this latitude ever extend over 12 inches [30 cm] or under 9 inches [23 cm]. The minimum limits do not apply to puppies. **Proportion**—The body from the forward-most point of the chest to the point of rump is 1/4 longer than the height at the withers. The body from the withers to lowest point of chest represents 1/2 the distance from withers to ground.

Substance—Compact and of medium bone throughout; neither coarse nor fine.

Head

Expression—Soft, dark-eyed, inquisitive, alert. **Eyes** are round, black or dark brown and are set in the skull to look directly forward. An overly large or bulging eye is a fault as is an almond shaped, obliquely set eye. Halos, the black or very dark brown skin surrounding the eyes, are necessary as they accentuate the eye and enhance expression. The eye rims themselves must be black. Broken pigment, or total absence of pigment on the eye rims produce a blank and staring expression, which is a definite fault. Eyes of any color other than black or dark brown are a very serious fault and must be severely penalized. **Ears** are drop and are covered with long flowing hair. When extended toward the nose, the leathers reach approximately halfway the length of the muzzle. They are set on slightly higher than eye level and rather forward on the skull, so that when the dog is alert they serve to frame the face. The **skull** is slightly rounded, allowing for a round and forward looking eye. The **stop** is slightly accentuated. **Muzzle**—A properly balanced head is three parts muzzle to five parts skull, measured from the nose to the stop and from the stop to the occiput. A line drawn between the outside corners of the eyes and to the nose will create a near equilateral triangle. There is a slight degree of chiseling under the eyes, but not so much as to result in a weak or snipey foreface. The lower jaw is strong. The **nose** is prominent and always black. **Lips** are black, fine, never drooping. **Bite** is scissors. A bite which is undershot or overshot should be severely penalized. A crooked or out of line

Ch. Special Times Just Rights is awarded Best in Show at the prestigious Westminster Kennel Club's show held at Madison Square Garden on Valentine's Day 2001.

tooth is permissible, however, missing teeth are to be severely faulted.

Neck, Topline, and Body

The arched **neck** is long and carried proudly behind an erect head. It blends smoothly into the shoulders. The length of neck from occiput to withers is approximately ⅓ the distance from forechest to buttocks. The **topline** is level except for a slight, muscular arch over the loin. **Body**—The chest is well developed and wide enough to allow free and unrestricted movement of the front legs. The lowest point of the chest extends at least to the elbow. The rib cage is moderately sprung and extends back to a short and muscular loin. The forechest is well pronounced and protrudes slightly forward of the point of shoulder. The underline has a moderate tuck-up. **Tail**

How the Bichon Differs from the Maltese and the Poodle

As we have noted in the Bichon's early history, the breed descended from the same rootstock that produced not only the other varieties of Bichon, but the Maltese and the Poodle as well. Be clear that the Bichon Frise is not the result of a cross between the Maltese and the Toy Poodle. Our Bichon Frise is a descendant of the same rootstock that produced the other two breeds. In other words, the three are "cousins," all tracing back to the same ancestors. As the three breeds journeyed along from their earliest origins, definite breed characteristics evolved. The distinguishing major differences are as follows:

Maltese

Coat: the Maltese coat is "single;" that is without any woolly undercoat. It hangs long, flat, and silky over the sides of the body, most often to the ground. The hair may not be kinky, curly, or woolly. There is no shaving and little scissoring of the coat.

Color: pure white, light tan, or lemon on ears is permissible but not desirable.

Size: weight under 7 pounds (3 kg), with 4 to 6 pounds (1.8–2.7 kg) preferred. No specification is given for height.

Toy Poodle

Coat: curly, of a naturally harsh texture, dense throughout. Presented at dog shows in standard prescribed clips, usually with the face, base of tail, and feet shaved and the remainder clipped to a specific pattern.

Color: solid colors only to include blues, grays, silvers, browns, cafe-au-laits, apricot, and cream, which are in reality only dilutions of black, white, and brown.

Size: weight is not considered; requirement is that it is 10 inches tall (25.6 cm) or less measured at the highest point of shoulder.

Bichon Frise

Coat: undercoat is soft and dense, the outercoat of a coarser and curlier texture. The combination of the two feels soft but substantial. When bathed and brushed the coat stands off the body like a powder puff. The coat is trimmed to reveal the natural outline of the body.

Color: color is white, but there may be shadings of buff, cream, or apricot around the ears and on the body. No off-white color in excess of 10 percent of the entire coat is allowed on a mature specimen.

Size: 9.5 to 11.5 inches (24.36–29.4 cm) measured at the shoulder is considered the ideal size range; no weight requirements given.

is well plumed, set on level with the topline and curved gracefully over the back so that the hair of the tail rests on the back. When the tail is extended toward the head it reaches at least halfway to the withers. A low tail set, a tail carried perpendicularly to the back, or a tail which droops behind is to be severely penalized. A corkscrew tail is a very serious fault.

Forequarters

Shoulders—The shoulder blade, upper arm, and forearm are approximately equal in length. The shoulders are laid back to somewhat near a forty-five degree angle. The upper arm extends well back so the elbow is placed directly below the withers when viewed from the side. **Legs** are of medium bone; straight, with no bow or curve in the forearm or wrist. The elbows are held close to the body. The **pasterns** slope slightly from the vertical. The dewclaws may be removed. The **feet** are tight and round, resembling those of a cat and point directly forward, turning neither in nor out. **Pads** are black. Nails are kept short.

Hindquarters

The hindquarters are of medium bone, well angulated with muscular thighs and spaced moderately wide. The upper and lower thigh are nearly equal in length meeting at a well bent stifle joint. The leg from hock joint to foot pad is perpendicular to the ground. Dewclaws may be removed. Paws are tight and round with black pads.

Coat

The texture of the coat is of utmost importance. The undercoat is soft and dense, the outercoat is of a coarser and curlier texture. The combination of the two gives a soft but substantial feel to the touch which is similar to plush or velvet and when patted springs back. When bathed and brushed, it stands off the body, creating an overall powder puff appearance. A wiry coat is not desirable. A limp, silky coat, a coat that lies down, or a lack of undercoat are very serious faults. **Trimming**—The coat is trimmed to reveal the natural outline of the body. It is rounded off from any direction and never cut so short as to create an overly trimmed or squared off appearance. The furnishings of the head, beard, moustache, ears, and tail are left longer. The longer head hair is trimmed to create an overall rounded impression. The topline is trimmed to appear level. The coat is long enough to maintain the powder puff look which is characteristic of the breed.

Color

Color is white, may have shadings of buff, cream, or apricot around the ears or on the body. Any color in excess of 10% of the entire coat of a mature specimen is a fault and should be penalized, but color of the accepted shadings should not be faulted in puppies.

Gait

Movement at a trot is free, precise, and effortless. In profile the forelegs and hind legs extend equally with an easy reach and drive that maintain a steady topline. When moving, the head and neck remain somewhat erect and as speed increases there is a very slight convergence of legs toward the center line. Moving away, the hindquarters travel with moderate width between them and the foot pads can be seen. Coming and going, his movement is precise and true.

Temperament

Gentle mannered, sensitive, playful, and affectionate. A cheerful attitude is the hallmark of the breed and one should settle for nothing less.

There are few subjects for the photographer's art that have greater appeal than a litter of puppies snuggled together and fast asleep in a wicker basket or gift box. Do understand, however, that a puppy will spend only a very small part of its day duplicating that serene picture.

All puppies are cuddly and cute and may even spend part of their day duplicating those appealing greeting card and calendar poses. The puppy will spend a far greater part of the day and night investigating, digging, chewing, eating, relieving itself, needing to go outdoors, and then immediately insisting that it be let back in. All too often these needs are not considered realistically before adding a dog to one's household.

Commitment to Dog Ownership

Many times the enticing pictures on greeting cards and calendars everywhere are what inspire well-meaning individuals to rush out

Dog ownership entails a great deal of commitment. It is very important that the prospective dog owner give sufficient consideration to the decision and never do so on a whim or because it was someone else's "good idea."

and buy a puppy for themselves or as a gift for a friend or loved one. The list of the real needs of a young puppy or an adult dog can be staggering to the uninitiated, and it takes a very concerned and dedicated human being to fulfill these needs. This is to say nothing of the time required for the many lessons the person must teach a dog, puppy or adult, before it understands what it may and may not do.

Friends often seek our advice when they are contemplating the purchase of their first dog. If we detect even the slightest uncertainty on their part, we always advise them to wait until they are absolutely sure they want to take on this great responsibility. Owning a dog takes great commitment and should never be done on a whim. The hasty purchase of a dog can result in sheer drudgery and frustration for the owner and an unhappy situation for the dog itself.

Failure to understand the amount of time and consideration a well-cared-for dog requires is one of the primary reasons many unwanted canines end their lives in an animal shelter. Given

It is very important that the prospective buyer understands the personality of the dog that will become a member of the family for many years. The Bichon Frise has an amiable personality but is not a dog for the heavy-handed or stern disciplinarian.

proper consideration beforehand, the purchase of a dog can bring a person many years of companionship and comfort as well as unconditional love and devotion no other animal can match.

In addition to these three major questions about dog ownership, it behooves the prospective dog owner to strongly consider the specific peculiarities of his or her own lifestyle or household. All this applies whether the household is made up of a single individual or a large family. Everyone involved must realize that the new dog will not understand the household routine and must be taught everything you want it to know and do.

This takes time and patience, and very often the most important lessons for the new dog to learn will take the longest for it to absorb.

Selecting a Purebred Dog

By buying a purebred puppy the purchaser will have a very good idea of what the dog will look like and even more important, how it will behave as an adult. Purebred dogs have been bred for generations to meet specifications of conformation and temperament.

When choosing a puppy, one must have the adult dog in mind, because the adult dog should fit the owner's lifestyle and aesthetic standards. A fastidious housekeeper may have trouble accommodating a large breed that sheds its coat year-round. Joggers or long-distance runners who want a dog to accompany them are not going be happy with a short-legged or slow breed. It is also important to know that short-muzzled dogs and those with "pushed-in" faces have very little heat tolerance. These are things that must be considered before you select a puppy.

Because the conformation of purebred dogs is entirely predictable, the owner of a purebred puppy will know whether the breed selected will still be appropriate as an adult. Temperament in purebred dogs has great predictability, although it might vary slightly within a breed. The hair-trigger response and hyperactivity of certain breeds would not be at all suitable for someone who wants a quiet, contented companion, nor would the placid attitude of yet other breeds be desirable for someone who wants an athletic, exuberant dog to frolic with. With purebred dogs, you are reasonably assured of selecting a dog compatible with your lifestyle.

CHECKLIST

Should You Own a Dog?

Three very important questions:

1. Does the person who will ultimately be responsible for the dog's day-to-day care really want a dog?

In many active families the mother of the household is the person who will have the ultimate responsibility for the family dog. She may not want any more duties than she already has. Pet care can be an excellent way to teach children responsibility, but beware—in their enthusiasm to have a puppy, children are apt to promise almost anything. It is what will happen after the novelty of a new dog has worn off that must be considered.

2. Does the lifestyle and schedule of the household lend itself to the demands of proper dog care?

This means there must always be someone available to see to the dog's basic needs: feeding, exercise, coat care, access to the outdoors when required, and the like.

3. Is the kind of dog being considered suitable for the individual or household?

Young children can unknowingly be very rough and unintentionally hurt a young puppy of a small breed. On the other hand, a young dog of a large breed can overwhelm and sometimes injure an infant or small child in an overly enthusiastic moment. Sharing a tiny apartment with a giant breed can prove extremely difficult for both dog and owner. Toy breeds will have difficulty surviving northern winters if required to live outdoors in unheated quarters. A long-haired dog, although attractive, is hardly suitable for the individual who spends most outdoor time camping, hunting, or hiking through the woods.

The initial purchase price of a purebred dog will be a significant investment for the owner, but a purebred dog costs no more to maintain than a mixed breed. If the cost of having exactly the kind of dog you want and are proud to own is gauged over the number of years you will enjoy it, you will have to admit the initial cost becomes far less consequential.

Before hastily buying a breed of dog whose *appearance* you find appealing, spend time with adult members of the breed or do some good research to assure yourself that you and the breed in question are temperamentally compatible. Many books have been written about various breeds, and they often devote a good amount of space to discussing the breed's temperament and compatibility. Visiting kennels or breeders specializing in the breed of your choice will assist you enormously in deciding if you are considering the right one for you.

Obviously people who breed and own a particular breed hold it in high regard or they would not be so involved. The question that must be answered is whether or not that particular breed is suitable for you.

All puppies are cute but they grow up to be adults that require a great deal of care and commitment. Dogs, unlike children, never arrive at the stage when they can do for themselves.

Is the Bichon Frise the Right Dog for Me?

The entire history of the Bichon Frise has been one of constant and close association with people. The Bichon has been the sailor's companion, favorite of royal families, circus performer, and war refugee.

This incredible versatility and hardiness makes the Bichon Frise one of the most adaptable of all breeds. The Bichon is suitable for an amazingly wide variety of living situations. First, the breed is a good size—neither too large for the smallest apartment, nor so small as to be at risk in a household of growing children.

The AKC standard of the breed says the size of the Bichon Frise should fall somewhere within the limits of 9.5 to 11.5 inches (24–29 cm) when measured at the shoulder. The average size for the breed is probably around 10.5 inches (27 cm). Some individuals are smaller at maturity and others a bit larger than average, but experienced breeders are able to predict roughly where on the size spectrum an individual Bichon puppy will fall at maturity.

Of the many breeds that we have owned and bred we can honestly say the Bichon is one of the most amiable. The breed can be equally at home with children and with the elderly. A Bichon is easily compatible with breeds much larger than itself as well as the tiniest of toy

Digging in the garden has great appeal for the Bichon, especially after a bath!

breeds. Introduced early enough, even cats can be the Bichon's friend and companion.

The Bichon Frise in full show trim may look like a fragile stuffed toy to some, but that look is entirely deceiving. Under the well-groomed coat is a sturdy, agile, and sound little dog that is constructed to keep up easily with the most active youngster or adult. One must not forget the Bichon's "street dog" heritage. This is a breed that historically has had to handle itself in all kinds of situations. Always ready for a good romp, a long hike, or a sensible jog in the park, the Bichon is not hyperactive and overly excitable and is equally content to spend a quiet afternoon or evening with an owner who is in a contemplative mood.

The Bichon is a built-in alarm system. The breed is very protective of its home and territory and will sound the alarm when necessary, yet is not prone to excessive barking.

A much-appreciated attribute of this breed is its practically odor-free and nonshedding coat. That in itself is a major consideration for a lot of people who object to a lifetime of sweeping, vacuuming the house, and brushing hair off clothing.

Other Considerations

As adaptable and amiable as the Bichon is, there are other criteria to be weighed. The freshly bathed and groomed Bichon certainly presents an attractive picture, but as exhibitors and breeders are inclined to say, "They look that way for about five minutes." The Bichon appears

The Bichon makes a wonderful companion for children who are old enough and responsible enough to understand how their pet should be treated.

══════ TIP ══════

Why a Purebred Dog?
There is no difference in the love, devotion, and companionship that a mixed-breed dog and a purebred dog can give its owner. There are, however, some aspects of suitability that can best be fulfilled by the purebred dog.

All puppies, purebred or not, are cute, but it stands to reason that not all puppies will grow up to be particularly attractive adults. It is nearly impossible to predict what a mixed-breed puppy will look like at maturity. Size, length of hair, and temperament can vary widely and may not be at all what the owner hopes for. What happens to the dog then?

Male or Female?

Although some individuals may prefer one sex over the other, we can honestly say that the male and the female Bichon Frise are pretty much equal in their intelligence and level of affection. The decision will have more to do with the owner's lifestyle and ultimate plans than differences between the sexes in the breed.

The Bichon Frise is one of our most adaptable breeds and can easily fit into many different lifestyles.

to be the eternal child and loves playing in the mud and digging holes as much as any human youngster. This can wreak havoc on that white, curly coat, and a Bichon seems to find that the best time for a romp in the mud is right after a bath. Although the Bichon coat does not shed, it does mat and tangle and requires regular bathing, trimming, and grooming to maintain that jaunty, tailored look that is a major part of its attraction. The pet owner should plan on devoting at least 20 to 30 minutes twice a week to keeping the Bichon tangle-free.

The breed's need of trimming will require either learning to do it properly yourself or employing the services of a professional groomer. We have included a chapter called "Bathing and Grooming" for those who wish to become proficient in this area. With time, practice, and the right grooming tools, the art can be mastered.

Some good professionals charge a hefty fee for their services, but owners who insist that their Bichon maintain the very special look of the breed find the results well worth it. Bichon owners must be prepared either to put in a fair amount of work on their dogs each week or budget the funds to have a professional do the work. Professional groomers charge about $50–$75 for a bath and pet-type trim, depending upon the part of the country and city in which the work is being done. A trim that equips a Bichon Frise to step into the show ring costs considerably more.

The Bichon appears to be generally nonallergic to humans, but like a good many white, pink-skinned dogs, the breed can be extremely flea sensitive. If ignored, this sensitivity can lead to severe scratching and skin eruptions called hot spots accompanied by hair loss.

The value of purchasing a purebred dog is that the owner will know just what his pet will grow up to look like as an adult.

Careful owners can, however, avoid these problems by constant surveillance and prevention. There are many commercial flea-exterminating services that will come to your home periodically and spray the premises, both indoor and out, thus assuring you of keeping the problem under control.

Female Bichons can be a bit slower to learn their housebreaking lessons than their brothers, but some males can prove to be problematic as well. The male of any breed of dog has a natural instinct to lift his leg and urinate on objects to establish and "mark" his territory. The degree of effort that must be invested in training the male not to do this varies with the individual dog. This habit becomes increasingly difficult to correct with the number of times a male dog is used for breeding. The mating act increases his need and desire to mark his territory.

On the other hand one must realize that the female will have her semiannual and sometimes burdensome heat cycle after she is eight or nine months old. At these times she must be confined to avoid soiling her surroundings, and she must be closely watched to prevent male dogs gaining access to her or she will become pregnant.

The sexually associated problems of housebreaking can be all but eliminated by having the pet Bichon "altered." Spaying the female and neutering the male will not change the character of your pet and will avoid the problems involved were you to choose not to do so. Neutering also precludes the possibility of your pet adding to the extreme pet overpopulation problem that concerns environmentalists worldwide.

It is important to understand though that these are not reversible procedures. If you are considering the possibility of showing your Bichon, altered animals are not allowed to compete in American Kennel Club conformation dog shows. Altered animals may, however, compete in obedience trials, agility events, and field trials.

Where to Buy Your Bichon

Your Bichon will live with you many years. This is a breed that regularly lives past 10, 12, and often 14 years of age. It is extremely important therefore that the dog you purchase comes from a source where physical and mental soundness are primary considerations in the breeding program. This is usually the result of careful breeding over many years. Selective

Most responsible breeders will have the litter mates and parents of the puppy you are interested in on the property. If possible it is wise to spend time with all your prospective puppy's relatives to get some sense of the canine family's personality.

breeding is aimed at maintaining the virtues of the breed and eliminating genetic weaknesses. Because it is time consuming and costly, good breeders protect their investment by providing the best prenatal care for their breeding females and the best nutrition for the growing puppies. There is no substitute for the amount of dedication and care good breeders give their dogs.

The Bichon Frise Club of America and the American Kennel Club can both provide the prospective buyer with the names and addresses of responsible individuals who have intelligently bred Bichons available for sale. Many local veterinarians carry a list of good breeders and can refer you directly to them as well.

The danger in buying a puppy from a pet shop is that the shop is usually the "middle man" in the transaction, the puppies having been born and raised elsewhere. The buyer usually has no idea what consideration was given to selecting the parents of the puppy, nor is there any way of finding out. Neither will the buyer have any knowledge of the environment in which the puppy was raised before it arrived at the pet shop or of what early care it was given.

There is a good chance that there are reputable breeders nearby who will be able to not only provide the Bichon you are looking for but advise you regularly about proper care and feeding. These breeders normally have the parents and other relatives of the Bichon you are interested in on the premises. The majority of them will be more than happy to have you see their dogs and to discuss the advantages and responsibilities involved in owning the breed. Responsible breeders are as concerned about their stock being placed in the right hands as you, the prospective buyer, are in having a sound and healthy dog.

Do not hesitate to ask questions and to ask to see the breeder's mature dogs. Experienced breeders know which hereditary problems exist in Bichons and will be happy to discuss them with you. Practically all breeds are subject to inherited ailments, and Bichons are no exception.

The temperament and health of the parents of your prospective purchase are of paramount importance. If you dislike what you observe in either of the parents, *look elsewhere!*

Inspect the environment in which the dogs are raised. Cleanliness is as important to producing good stock as good pedigrees are. The time you spend researching and inspecting the kennel and the adult dogs it houses may well save you a great deal of money and heartache in the years to come.

All this is not to imply that your Bichon puppy must come from a large kennel. On the contrary, many good puppies are produced by small hobby breeders in their homes. These names may well be included in recommendations from both the American Kennel Club and the Bichon Frise Club of America. These individuals offer the same investment of time, study, and knowledge as the larger kennel and are just as ready to offer the same health guarantees.

A newspaper advertisement may or may not lead you to a reputable hobby breeder. It is up to you to investigate and compare as you would in the case of any major purchase. Good hobby breeders sell only to approved buyers and spend considerable time in determining whether buyers are suitable. If the seller is willing to let you make a purchase with no questions asked, you should be highly suspicious.

HELPFUL HINT: Beware of breeders who tell you that their dogs are not susceptible to inherited diseases or potential problems. I do not mean to imply that all Bichons are afflicted with genetic problems, but a reliable breeder will give you the information you are entitled to about the individual Bichon you are considering. The chapter called "Veterinary Care and Inherited Problems" gives details on possible genetic ailments.

Although always ready for a romp in the park or hike in the hills, the Bichon can be just as content for indoor games on those rainy afternoons.

SELECTING A BICHON PUPPY

The Bichon you want to buy should be a happy, playful extrovert. Never select a puppy that appears frail or sickly because you feel sorry for him.

Bichon puppies with positive temperaments are not afraid of strangers. Under normal circumstances you will have the whole litter in your lap if you kneel and call them to you. Avoid the puppy that cowers in a corner and tries to run away from you.

If one puppy in particular appeals to you, pick him up and, if possible, carry him off to an area nearby where the two of you can spend some time alone. As long as a puppy is still in a fairly familiar environment where scents and sounds are not entirely strange, he should retain his outgoing personality.

Veterinary Health Check

Most breeders are more than happy to supply a written agreement that the sale of a puppy is contingent upon the puppy's successfully passing

When purchasing your Bichon puppy realize that he or she will be a member of the family for many years to come.

a veterinary health check. If the location of the breeders, your home, and your prospective veterinarian allow it, plan the time of day you pick up your puppy so that you can go directly from the breeder to the veterinarian. If this is not possible, you should plan the visit as soon as possible. No longer than 24 hours should elapse before this is done. Should the puppy not pass the veterinary health check, a responsible breeder will be more than happy either to refund your money or provide you with another puppy.

If you have been reading and doing your research, you can expect the Bichon puppy to look almost like a miniaturized version of an adult, aside from the length and texture of coat. Bichon puppies have very soft coats, nothing like the firm, "powder puff" texture required for adults.

Best Age for Selection

Raising a puppy is a wonderful experience. Granted, at times it can also be one of the

Quick Health Check

When you and your prospective puppy are alone, you will have an opportunity to examine the puppy more closely. Check the puppy's ears. They should be pink and clean. Any odor or dark discharge could indicate ear mites, which in turn could indicate poor maintenance. The inside of the mouth and gums should also be pink, and the teeth should be clean and white. There should be no malformation of the mouth or jaw. The dark eyes should be clear and bright. Again, be aware of any signs of discharge.

As small as Bichon puppies are, they should feel compact and substantial to the touch, never bony and undernourished, or bloated. A taut, bloated abdomen is usually a sign of worms. However, a *rounded* puppy belly is normal. The nose of a Bichon puppy should not be crusted or running. A cough or diarrhea is a danger signal, as are any kinds of eruptions on the skin.

Conformation is important even at an early age. The Bichon puppy's legs should be straight. As the pup walks toward you, its front legs should move directly forward, as should the rear legs when the pup is moving away from you. The movement should be free and easy.

most exasperating projects you have ever attempted. In the end, though, having endured each other through all the trials of puppyhood, you and your Bichon will forge a bond that has no equal.

Should you decide that you do in fact wish to raise this bit of fluff from infancy to adulthood, be aware that most breeders do not and should not release their puppies until they have had their initial inoculations, which is at about eight to ten weeks of age. Do not remove a puppy from its home environment before it has been vaccinated.

Before immunization, puppies are very susceptible to infectious diseases. Many such diseases may be transmitted via people's clothing and hands. After the first series of vaccinations the breeder will inform you when your Bichon puppy is ready to leave its first home.

Show Dog or Companion?

If dog shows and breeding are in your Bichon puppy's future, you should know that the older he is at time of selection, the more likely you are to know how good a dog you will have at maturity. The most any breeder can say about an eight-week-old Bichon puppy is that he has or does not have "show potential." If you are seriously interested in having a Bichon of the quality to show or to breed, wait with your selection until the puppy is at least five to six months old. By this time you can be far more certain of dentition, soundness, and attitude, as well as other important characteristics. No matter what you have in mind for your Bichon's future—dog shows or nothing more than loving companionship—all of the foregoing about health and soundness should be considered carefully.

If the excitement and pride of owning a winning show dog appeals to you, we cannot urge you enough to seek out a successful breeder who has a record of having produced winning dogs through the years. As noted above, it is

The length of your puppy's body might be a determining factor for a future show dog.

extremely difficult, if not impossible, to predict what an eight-week-old puppy will look like as an adult. An experienced breeder, however, will know whether a young puppy has "potential." Unfortunately most prospective owners want both a very young puppy and some guarantee that the puppy will grow up to be a winning show dog. It is not possible to give that kind of guarantee, and no honest breeder will do so.

Show-Prospect Puppies

A show-prospect puppy must not only adhere to all the health and soundness qualifications of the good pet puppy, but must show every sign that it will conform very closely to the rigid demands of the breed standard when it matures. It might make little difference to you if your pet is a bit longer in body or shorter on leg than what the breed standard considers ideal, but faults like this make considerable difference in determining the future of a show dog.

All male show dogs must have two normal-sized testicles in the scrotum. Some males have only one testicle, and this eliminates them from being considered as a show prospect. Certainly this would make no difference to pet owners who will have their male dogs sexually altered anyway. Therefore purchasing a male with this "fault" could give the buyer a beautiful dog that might otherwise not be affordable.

We have known some people who have spent thousands of dollars buying very young Bichon puppies again and again but have never achieved their goal of owning a winning show dog. Granted, an older puppy or grown dog may initially cost considerably more than an

eight-week-old puppy, but odds are much greater that in the end you will have what you actually wanted.

Experienced and successful Bichon breeders have spent years developing a line of top-quality animals. These breeders know what to look for in the breed and are particularly familiar

The young Bichon Frise puppy is small but should feel substantial when you hold one.

TIP

Experience Counts

Your chances of obtaining a Bichon puppy that will mature into a winning adult are far better if purchased from a breeder whose Bichon bloodline has produced many champions. Even at that, no one can be sure of having a winner until the puppy has reached maturity. Obviously a puppy six or seven months old or a young adult will provide much more certainty.

with the manner in which their own stock matures. It is important to understand that although a show dog will provide the same amount of love and devotion as one purchased strictly as a pet, you will have a great deal more work in coat care and maintenance.

Price

The price of a Bichon puppy can vary considerably, but buyers should understand that reputable breeders have invested considerable time, skill, and work to make sure they have the best possible breeding stock. This costs a great deal of money. Good breeders have also invested substantially in veterinary supervision and testing to keep their stock as free from hereditary defects as possible.

A puppy purchased from an established and successful breeder may cost a few dollars more initially, but the small additional investment can save many trips to the veterinarian over the ensuing years. It is heartbreaking to become attached to a dog only to lose him at an early age because of some health defect.

You should expect to pay at least $1,000–$1,500 or more for an eight-week-old, pet-quality puppy. Older puppies will cost considerably more. Youngsters with show and breeding potential will be again more expensive.

Inoculations and Health Certificates

By 12 weeks of age most puppies have been vaccinated against hepatitis, leptospirosis, distemper, and canine parvovirus. Rabies inoculations are usually not given until the puppy is six months of age. There is a set series of inocula-

A puppy is not the only option for the prospective owner. Often young adults are available that will avoid having to go through all the problems of puppyhood.

tions developed to combat these infectious diseases; more details are given in the chapter "Veterinary Care and Inherited Problems."

You are entitled to have a record of these inoculations when you purchase your Bichon. Most breeders will give you complete documentation, along with dates on which your puppy was wormed and examined by the veterinarian. Usually this record will also indicate when "booster" shots are required. These are very important records to keep; the veterinarian you choose for the care of your Bichon will need them.

Pedigree and Registration Certificate

Buying a purebred dog also entitles you to a copy of the dog's pedigree and registration certificate. These are two separate documents. The former is simply the dog's family tree. It lists the registered names of your Bichon's sire and dam along with their ancestors for several generations.

The American Kennel Club issues the registration certificate. When ownership of your Bichon is transferred from the breeder's name to your name, the transaction is entered on this certificate, and once mailed to the AKC it is permanently recorded in their computerized records. The AKC will send you a copy of the duly recorded change. File this document in a safe place along with your other important papers, as you will need it should you ever wish to show or breed your Bichon.

If the buyer has a future show dog in mind, it is important to remember that the older the puppy the better that predictability is.

Responsible breeders make a considerable investment in making sure their stock is as free from hereditary defects as possible. Their dedication ensures your purchase will provide a minimal number of health problems.

Your Bichon will keep a look out for strangers and will be sure to sound the alarm if he thinks something is not quite right.

Diet Sheet

A sound and healthy Bichon puppy is in that condition because he has been properly fed and cared for. Every breeder has a slightly different approach to successful nutrition, so it is wise to obtain a written record or description that details the amount and kind of food your puppy has been receiving. It should also indicate the number of times a day your Bichon puppy has been accustomed to being fed and the kind of vitamin supplementation he has been receiving, if any. Maintaining this system at least for the first week or two after your puppy comes home with you will reduce the chances of digestive upsets and loose stools. A good dietary program also projects increases in food and changes that should be made in the dog's diet as he matures.

Consider an Adult Bichon

A very young puppy is not your only option for adding a Bichon to your household. For some people, especially the elderly, a housebroken adult can be an excellent choice. Also, if time available to housebreak is limited or the owner expects to be away from home frequently, an adult Bichon can be a wise choice.

Practically all Bichons, even adults, seem to adapt to their new environments very easily. This cannot be said for all other breeds. The mature Bichon also needs far less supervision than a puppy, because it has normally passed through the mischievous stage and the need to chew. Usually an adult Bichon is ready, willing, and *capable* of learning the household routine.

Another factor to consider is that some adult Bichons may never have been exposed to or interacted with little children. If there are young children in your home, the inexperienced Bichon may find the first sight of these "miniature people" perplexing and frightening. It may take time and patience to overcome initial fears, but with perseverance and good judgment it is usually not too difficult a task. Most Bichons I have observed have a natural affinity with children.

Giving the adult Bichon not used to small children an area of its own where the children are excluded is vitally important. An adult Bichon nearly always comes around and accepts children when it is ready, but if children continually rush up to grab the dog or, worse yet, chase after it, this simply reinforces the fearful behavior.

HELPFUL HINT: There are some important things to consider in bringing an adult Bichon into your home. The adult dog may have developed habits that you do not find acceptable. In some cases it may be difficult to retrain such animals. Until you begin to work together, there is no way of knowing how willing an adult Bichon is to learn new habits. Always take an adult dog home on a trial basis to see how it works out for both you and the dog.

Bichons love playing games and will join in with the family at the slightest invitation.

It may take special care to introduce the adult Bichon to children if the dog has not been accustomed to them.

CARE OF THE BICHON PUPPY

There is a great deal you can do before your Bichon puppy's arrival to make the transition as painless and trauma-free as possible. If possible, visit your puppy several times while it is still in its original home so that you are not entirely a stranger.

Preparing for the New Puppy

Well in advance of the puppy's arrival you can secure the equipment and toys that will be needed and prepare the area in which it will live initially. A fenced-off area in the kitchen is the ideal place to start your puppy off; accidents can be easily cleaned up and there is normally a good deal of traffic. Don't forget, a young puppy is accustomed to the companionship of its littermates. Without them the puppy will be lonely. It will be up to you to compensate for the loss of your puppy's siblings.

Equipment and Toys

The following is a list of the basic requirements you should already have satisfied by the time your puppy arrives. The value and use of each will be more fully explained as we proceed.

A new arrival shopping list is a must.

Partitioned-off living area: Paneled fence partitions about 3 feet (92 cm) high are available at most major pet shops and are well worth the investment for keeping the puppy where you want it to be. Bichon puppies love to be where their owners are, but underfoot is not where a puppy should be.

Cage or shipping kennel: Inside the fenced-off area there should be a wire cage or fiberglass shipping kennel (the open door of which provides access to a sleeping "den"). This cage will also be used for housebreaking. The cage housebreaking method is explained in detail later in this chapter. These wire cages and fiberglass shipping kennels come in varying sizes. The medium size (approximately 20 inches [51 cm] high by 24 inches [61 cm] wide by 30 inches [77 cm] long) will be the ideal size to accommodate your Bichon even as an adult.

Water dish and feeding bowl: These are available in many different materials. Choose

CHECKLIST

Basic Needs for Your Puppy's Arrival

✔ Partitioned-off living area
✔ Cage or shipping kennel
✔ Water dish and feeding bowl
✔ Recommended puppy food
✔ Brush and comb
✔ Soft collar and leash
✔ Toys

something nonbreakable and hard to tip over. Bichon puppies very quickly learn to upset the water bowl and relish turning their entire living area into a swimming pool! We recommend plastic or stainless steel bowls because they eliminate the worry of toxic content.

Food as recommended on the diet sheet obtained from your puppy's breeder: In the unlikely circumstance that you were not provided with this information, there are many highly nutritious commercial brands of dog food available at pet stores and supermarkets that come complete with feeding instructions. Veterinarians are always helpful in this area as well.

Brush and comb: A young Bichon's coat does not require a great deal of grooming, but the process should begin early. Equipment that you will need is described in detail in the chapter called "Bathing and Grooming."

Soft collar and a leash: These should be very lightweight and are what you will need to begin initial lead training.

Toys: These can be anything you choose, but be sure they are safe—without buttons or strings that can be chewed off or swallowed. Also avoid hard plastic toys that can splinter. Make sure all toys are larger than those that the puppy can get into its mouth. Small toys can become lodged in the mouth and caught in the throat. Do not give your Bichon puppy old, discarded shoes or stockings to play with. A puppy is unable to determine the difference between "old" and "new" and unless carefully watched may think it is perfectly all right to add newly acquired $100 jogging shoes to its toy collection.

Obtaining the basic equipment before your puppy arrives gives the newcomer a safe little haven of its own. Here the new puppy rests in its crate, enclosed in portable, partitioned fencing. Water bowl, food dish, and play toys are easily accessible. The only thing else the puppy needs is your love.

Bringing Your Puppy Home

The safest way to transport the puppy from the kennel to your home is to obtain a pet carrier or cardboard box large enough for the puppy to stretch out comfortably, with sides high enough so that it cannot climb out. Put a layer of newspapers at the bottom in case of accidents and a soft blanket or towel on top of that. Ideally another family member or friend will be able to accompany you to do the driving or hold the carrier.

Do not give your Bichon puppy discarded personal items like shoes or articles of clothing. They have your smell as do new items and a dog has no sense of "old" or "new."

Socialization and Safety

It is important that you accustom the Bichon puppy to everyday events as soon as it is practical. Strange noises, children, and other animals can be very frightening when the puppy first encounters them.

Some breeders make it a point to expose their puppies to as many everyday sights and sounds as possible, but this is not always practical when many dogs have to be taken care of. Therefore it is up to you to gently and gradually introduce your puppy to such sounds as the garbage disposal, the vacuum cleaner, and the television set.

Ideally the first time your puppy is exposed to a strange, loud sound you will be able to keep the sound limited to just a few seconds. Once the puppy learns the sound does not present danger, you will be able to increase the length of time. Eventually the puppy will take even the loudest sounds in stride.

The Bichon Frise is a gardener at heart. Just make sure what is being transplanted is what you had in mind.

Bichon puppies can find their way into places in which they might be hurt or in which they could damage valuable property. It is important to "puppy-proof" your home before your puppy arrives.

HELPFUL HINT: When your puppy arrives at its new home, it will be confused and undoubtedly whine in search of its litter-mates. This will be especially so at night when there are no littermates to snuggle up to. For the first few nights after the new puppy arrives we put a box next to the bed and let the newcomer sleep there. Should the puppy wake up crying in loneliness, a reassuring hand can be dropped into the box and we avoid having to trudge to a different part of the house to quiet the lonely puppy.

Letting the puppy "howl it out" can be a nerve-racking experience that could easily cost you, your family, and your neighbors nights of sleep. Should you wish to transfer the puppy's sleeping quarters to a different part of the house later, you can do this more easily once the puppy has acclimated to the new surroundings and learned to be by itself for increasing periods of time.

We previously mentioned that children can be very frightening to the adult Bichon that has never spent time with "little humans." This applies to puppies as well. Although many young Bichons innately love children, there are exceptions in which they at first frighten puppies with no previous exposure to children. Supervising introductions is very important. A quiet, gentle approach on the child's part normally leads to establishing a lasting friendship, and soon dog and child form a lasting bond.

Regardless of whether the Bichon puppy has had prior experience with young children, the children themselves must be educated about what they may and may not do with the new puppy. Learning the gentle approach, exercising caution when the puppy is underfoot, and taking care not to make loud and sudden noises are all lessons that the adult should teach young children as part of responsible dog ownership.

"Puppy-Proofing" Your Home

A good part of your Bichon puppy's safety depends upon your ability to properly "puppy-proof" your home. Electrical outlets, lamp cords, strings, and mouth-size objects of any kind all spell danger to the inquisitive Bichon puppy. If you think of your new arrival as one part building inspector and one part vacuum cleaner, you will be better equipped to protect your puppy from itself.

Puppy biting and growling may be cute in the very young puppy, but such things should never be encouraged in that they can become hard to eliminate habits.

Bichon puppies can be ingenious at getting into places they shouldn't be. Items such as household cleaning products and gardening supplies should be kept in securely latched cupboards out of a puppy's reach.

There is a product called Bitter Apple that tastes just like it sounds—*terrible!* Actually a furniture cream, it is nonpoisonous and can be used to coat electrical wires and chair legs. In most (not all) cases it will deter puppies from damaging not only household items but themselves as well. Should Bitter Apple not work, plastic tubing is available at hardware stores that can be put around electrical cords and some furniture legs.

There are baby gates to keep your puppy out and cages and kennels of various kinds to keep your puppy in. All this and a daily "puppy-proofing patrol" will help you and your pet avoid serious damage and potential danger.

The New Puppy and Other Pets

The Bichon puppy's introduction to older and/or larger dogs in the household must also be carefully supervised. The average Bichon puppy loves the world and all creatures in it. The adult dog "with seniority," however, may consider the new youngster an intrusion and mistake its exuberance as aggression. For this reason it is important to confine the newcomer so that the older dog is not constantly harassed before it has had time to fully accept the puppy. The partitioned area set up to accommodate the new puppy that we described earlier will give the senior member of the canine contingent an opportunity to inspect the new arrival at his or her leisure without having to endure unsolicited attention.

As mentioned before, Bichons are among the most amiable dogs. We have seen them develop lasting friendships with dogs the size of Great Danes and St. Bernards and seen other Bichons take charge of and become very protective of little creatures such as kittens, hamsters, and small birds.

Car Travel

A part of a Bichon puppy's socialization process will take place away from home. The puppy must learn to accept strange people and places, and the only way for it to learn to take these changes in stride is to visit as many new sites and meet as many strangers as you can arrange. Trips to the shopping mall or walks through the park will expose your young

TIP

Lifting and Carrying Your Bichon

Learning to pick up and carry the Bichon puppy properly is very important for both adult and child. You should pick up the puppy with one hand supporting its rear and hindquarters and the other hand under the puppy's chest. This gives the puppy a feeling of security and enables you to keep full control. *A puppy should never be picked up by its front legs or by the scruff of the neck.*

Only children old enough to safely hold and control a puppy should be allowed to pick it up at all. Puppies can suddenly squirm and attempt to get away. A fall from any height can seriously and permanently injure a puppy.

Both children and adults should learn the proper way to pick up and carry a puppy—one hand supports the rear, the other hand is placed under the chest between the puppy's legs.

Bichon to new and different situations each time you are out. Of course this should never be attempted until your Bichon puppy has had all of its inoculations. Once that is completed, you and your puppy are ready to set off to meet the world. This often involves riding in a car.

Most adult Bichons love to ride in a car; the moment they hear those car keys jingle, they are ready and willing to go. Unfortunately, some puppies initially suffer varying degrees of motion sickness. The best way to overcome this problem is to begin with very short rides—as short as once around the block. End the ride with a fun romp, or, should the puppy be interested, give it a little food treat to help make the ride something to be enjoyed.

When the puppy seems to accept these short rides happily, the length of time in the car can be gradually increased until you see that the young Bichon is truly enjoying the outings. Even those dogs and puppies suffering the most severe cases of carsickness seem to respond to this approach and soon begin to consider the car a second home.

Words of Caution on Dogs and Cars

As much as it might seem more enjoyable to have your Bichon puppy or adult ride loose in the car, this can be extremely dangerous. An overly enthusiastic canine passenger can interfere with the driver's control or divert the driver's attention. Also a sudden stop can hurl your dog against the front window, severely injuring or even killing it.

The safest way to transport your Bichon is in a carrier with the door securely latched. There are also cars such as station wagons that accommodate partitions commonly referred to as dog guards. These safety devices confine dogs to the rear portion of the car. These simple safety precautions might one day save the life of your pet.

Another important travel tip is to make sure your canine companion is wearing a collar with identification tags attached. (In fact, whenever your Bichon is not at home with you, it should be wearing a collar with identification tags.) Many times dogs are thrown clear of the car in an accident but become so frightened they run blindly away. Not knowing where they are and without any means of identification, the dogs may be lost forever.

It is important that you never leave your Bichon alone in the car with the windows closed. Even on cool days the sun beating down on a closed car can send the inside temperature soaring. Though one would expect it to be more the case with black or dark-colored dogs, Bichons are extremely heat sensitive. On hot days most Bichons will do their best to avoid direct sunlight. Leaving a Bichon alone in an unventilated car could easily cause its death.

Early Training

Simple basic training should begin just as soon as you bring your puppy home. It must be remembered, however, that young puppies' attention spans are very short and that they are incapable of understanding or retaining complex commands.

It should also be noted here that Bichons as a breed are very sensitive to correction and that a scolding is usually sufficient to get your point across. Shaking or striking a Bichon is never necessary. Even the most persistent unwanted behavior can normally be taken care of by slapping a rolled-up newspaper on the floor and giving a sharp *"No!"*

Come

It is critical that your Bichon puppy learn to come when called. Therefore the puppy must learn her name as soon as possible. Learning to come when called *could well save your Bichon's life when the two of you venture out into the world.* A dog must understand that *"come"* has

Very young puppies know none of the household rules. Common sense may tell you that there are definite "no no's" that should be observed, but it is up to you to convince the youngster that this is important.

to be obeyed always and instantly, but the dog should not associate that command with fear. Your Bichon's responding to her name and the word *come* should always be associated with a pleasant experience such as great praise and

petting or a food treat. In dog training of any kind it is much easier to avoid the establishment of bad habits than it is to correct entrenched, undesirable behavior. Never give the *come* command unless you are sure your Bichon puppy will come to you. Initially, use the command when the puppy is already on its way to you or give the command while walking away from the youngster.

Very young puppies normally want to stay as close to their owners as possible, especially in strange surroundings. When a puppy sees its owner moving away, the natural inclination is to catch up. This is a perfect time to use the *come* command.

If you are not going to train your puppy to eliminate outdoors, newspapers on a tiled floor are another option.

Later, as your puppy grows more independent and perhaps a bit headstrong, you may want to attach a long leash or rope to her collar to ensure the correct response. Chasing or punishing your puppy for not obeying the *come* command in the initial training stages makes the youngster associate the command with something negative and will result in avoidance rather than the immediate positive response you desire. It is imperative that you praise your puppy when she does come to you, even if she delays responding for several minutes.

Leash Training

It is never too early to accustom your Bichon puppy to a collar and leash. It is your way of keeping your dog under control. It may not be necessary for the puppy or adult Bichon to wear a collar and identification tags within the confines of your home or securely fenced property, but no dog should ever leave home without a collar and without the leash held securely in your hand.

Begin getting your puppy accustomed to her collar by leaving it on for a few minutes at a time. Gradually extend the time you leave the collar on. Most puppies become accustomed to a collar very quickly and forget they are even wearing it.

Once this is accomplished, attach a lightweight leash to the collar while you are playing with the puppy in the house or in your yard. Do not try to guide her at first. The point here is to accustom the puppy to the feeling of having something attached to the collar. Encourage her to follow you as you move away. Should she be reluctant to cooperate, coax her along with a treat of some kind. Hold the treat in front of your puppy's nose to encourage her to

follow you. Just as soon as she takes a few steps toward you, praise her enthusiastically and do so as you continue to move along.

Make the initial session brief and enjoyable. Continue the lessons in your home or yard until your puppy is completely unconcerned about the fact that she is on a leash. With a treat in one hand and the leash in the other you can begin to use both to guide her in the direction you wish to go.

Once the collar and leash are being taken in stride, you can begin your walks in front of the house, then down the street, and eventually around the block. You and your Bichon puppy are on your way to a lifetime of adventure.

A comfortable collar with leash attached are your Bichon's best friend because they insure control and help avoid dangerous situations.

HOW-TO: HOUSEBREAK

Using a crate reduces the average housebreaking time to a minimum and eliminates keeping the puppy under constant stress by correcting it for making mistakes in the home.

Confining your puppy is the only possible way to avoid soiling accidents in the house. Most dogs are instinctively clean and will not soil their immediate surroundings unless they have no choice. That said, once a dog has eliminated in a particular place, even within the home, that spot becomes a "free zone," an okay spot to return to when nature calls.

The Crate Method

The crate used for housebreaking should not be too large or your puppy will sleep at one end and eliminate in the other. It should be large enough for the puppy to stretch out comfortably as

The "crate method" of housebreaking can be one of the most valuable training procedures you will use. It reduces housebreaking time to a minimum.

well as stand up and turn around easily.

Begin using the crate by feeding your puppy in it. Close and latch the door while the puppy is eating. Just as soon as the food has been consumed, unlatch the crate door and *carry* the puppy outdoors to the place where you want her to eliminate. Should you not have access to the outdoors or think you will later not be able to provide outdoor access for the housebroken dog, place newspapers or some other absorbent material in an out-of-the-way place that will remain easily accessible to the puppy. Do not let her run about or play after eating until you have carried her to the designated area. Again, remember that it will be extremely difficult to teach your Bichon puppy not to eliminate indoors once she has begun to do so. It is very important to take the time to prevent accidents rather than try to correct them after they have occurred.

Young puppies will void both bowel and bladder almost immediately after eating, after strenuous play, and upon waking up from a night's sleep or even a nap. If, after each of these activities, you consistently take the puppy to

the place designated for eliminating, you will reinforce the habit of going there for that purpose.

Only after seeing that your puppy has relieved herself in both ways should you allow her to play unconfined—and then only while you are there to watch what is happening. Should she begin to sniff the floor and circle around or squat down to relieve herself, say, "no!" pick her up immediately, and take her to the designated place.

When you are not able to watch what your puppy is doing indoors, she should be in the crate with the door latched. Each time you take her to her crate, throw a small food treat inside and praise the puppy as she enters the crate to go after the treat. If your puppy starts whining, barking, or scratching at the door because she wants to be let out, it is crucial that you do not submit to those demands. A puppy must learn not only to stay in her crate but also to do so without complaining unnecessarily.

Every time your puppy begins to whine or bark, say, "no!" very firmly. If necessary, give the crate a sharp rap with a rolled-up newspaper.

Developing a Schedule

It is important to realize that a puppy of 8 to 12 weeks will have to relieve her bladder every few hours except at night. You must adjust your schedule and the puppy's accordingly. You must also be sure your puppy has entirely relieved herself at night just before you retire and be prepared to attend to this the very first thing in the morning when you awake. Just how early your puppy needs her first outing in the morning will undoubtedly be determined by the puppy herself, but do not expect a young puppy to wait very long for you to respond to the "I have to go out now" signals.

Eventually you will begin to detect a somewhat anxious look or attitude in your puppy that indicates that she needs to relieve herself. Even the slightest indication in this direction should be met with immediate action on your part and accompanied with high praise and positive reinforcement.

When the Owner Is Away All Day

The crate method of housebreaking is without a doubt the simplest and quickest way I have ever found to housebreak the Bichon puppy. It is obvious, however, that it cannot be used by someone who is away from home all day or for even many hours at a time. Young puppies cannot contain themselves for long periods of time. An alternative method must be used, but *confinement* is still the operative word for success.

If you ever hope to complete the housebreaking task, a puppy should never be left to roam the house while you are away. It is dangerous for the puppy, and toilet accidents are bound to happen. Once the accident happens, you then have to have the puppy unlearn the bad habit before establishing the correct behavior. That can be extremely difficult with Bichons.

A sure sign the young puppy is preparing to relieve herself is when she begins to sniff the floor and circle around or squat.

The fenced-off area in the kitchen recommended for the arrival of the new puppy is the ideal place of confinement for your puppy while you are gone. The space should be only large enough to permit the puppy to eliminate away from the place in which it sleeps.

The floor of the fenced-off area should be lined with newspaper. This should become the "designated spot" to which you will take your puppy when you are home and she indicates it is time to eliminate. When you are home, you must insist that the puppy use the newspapers every time.

Housebreaking
When to Take Your Puppy Outdoors
(Or to the newspapers)
1. Very first thing in the morning
2. Immediately after eating
3. Immediately after drinking
4. Right after a nap
5. When she circles and sniffs the floor
6. Right after "playtime"
7. When she gets that "perplexed" look
8. When she starts to squat

Historically the Bichon Frise has been a close companion to people. Whether pampered in the courts of the nobility, living on the streets with vendors and entertainers, or treasured now as your friend, one thing has remained constant—the Bichon is always happiest in the company of its owner. This characteristic has been cultivated and perpetuated through selective breeding over many centuries.

Understanding Your Bichon

Some breeds do well living outdoors in a run or in a kennel with only minimal human contact. The Bichon is definitely not one of those breeds. The charming personality and sensitivity for which the breed is noted blossoms with constant human association. If the Bichon is left alone too often or for long periods of time, behavioral problems can develop.

It is not unusual to find a perfectly house-broken Bichon protest denial of human contact by forgetting all about house manners. Bichons that are not given the attention they need can become frustrated and begin to destroy things. More often than not this destruction focuses on personal objects belonging to the lonely Bichon's owner.

This does not mean people who are away at work or school all day cannot own a Bichon.

In addition to being your good friend a Bichon must learn to be a good canine citizen.

What it does mean is that you must plan on giving your Bichon high-quality attention and affection every day during the hours you are at home. This can come in the form of daily walks, playing retrieving games, grooming sessions, or simply having your Bichon sit beside you while you watch television or read in the evening hours.

A Passive Breed

Basically the Bichon can best be described as a passive rather than an assertive breed of dog. A more passive dog such as the Bichon prefers to stay at home or travel with its owner and is seldom what is referred to as a runaway or wanderer. Like most passive breeds the Bichon thoroughly enjoys exercise but does not become hyperactive and destructive if a day is missed. A Bichon barks to sound the alarm but quickly settles down and seldom if ever barks or growls as a sign of aggression.

Not everyone that you and your Bichon meet on the street is a dog lover. Be sure to keep your pal leashed and under control when you are out taking your daily strolls.

It is a rare Bichon that would challenge its owner on any point. The breed is most comfortable knowing the household rules and having an owner who makes sure the rules are enforced.

Exercise and Outdoor Manners

If your Bichon shares his life with another dog or with children, there is every likelihood that he will get as much exercise as he needs. Bichons love to romp and play and will attempt to entice almost any human or animal available to join in. In fact, even Bichons that have no playmates will invent games that result in keeping their cardiovascular systems in shape and any excess energy in check.

Do not think your Bichon would not enjoy a long walk with you every day; to the contrary. Most Bichons will willingly walk as far, and perhaps farther, than their owners wish to go. Regardless of how many playmates your Bichon has at home or how many games it plays on its own, a good brisk walk every day will contribute immensely toward keeping you both happy and healthy.

It is important to understand that although we have referred to the Bichon as one of the more passive breeds, we do not mean it is delicate or timid by any means. Don't forget, this

The Bichon Frise responds best to authoritative commands. Never strike your Bichon under any circumstance.

was a hardy street dog for many generations. The breed had to take care of itself in all kinds of weather and in all kinds of situations.

If you and your Bichon both keep moving, you need not worry about even the coldest of outdoor weather. The Bichon is a tough little breed, and its own furry jacket protects it from even freezing temperatures.

On the other hand, caution should be exercised during hot weather. Plan your walks for early morning or after the sun has gone down. Most Bichons do not like extremely hot weather and do their utmost to avoid direct sun when temperatures begin to soar.

You must remember to keep your Bichon under control at all times when you are out walking. Always use a leash and collar and make sure the identification tags are securely attached to the collar.

Remember that not all people are dog lovers and that even those who are may not appreciate strange dogs jumping up on them on the street. Short-leash your Bichon as you pass strangers. Only if the person indicates a desire to become friendlier with your dog should you allow your Bichon to approach the person.

Never let your dog relieve itself where people might walk or children are playing. Try to teach your Bichon to use the gutter to relieve itself. Even then you should always carry a small plastic bag to remove droppings immediately and dispose of them in a trash receptacle. Many city governments impose heavy fines on dog owners who do not pick up after their dogs.

Dealing with Problems

Most of the problems owners experience with their Bichons are caused by the owner rather than

Be firm but gentle in all you do with your Bichon. Daily grooming and health checks make your pet understand that there are certain things you require whether or not they are convenient for the little fellow.

HELPFUL HINT: The Bichon tries to please in all respects and is relatively easy to train just so long as you avoid being heavy-handed. Bichons are extremely sensitive to correction, and a simple scolding is usually more than sufficient to get your point across. Never strike your Bichon under any circumstance. Some breeds need a smart slap on the rear quarter with a rolled-up newspaper to get their attention, if nothing else. For Bichon's this is neither necessary nor advisable. Should the rolled-up newspaper technique ever be used to make a correction, the noise created by slapping the floor with the paper is more than enough to let your Bichon know you are displeased.

No matter how cute you may think your Bichon is, it is wise to remember that not all people are dog lovers. Allow visitors the opportunity to decide for themselves whether or not they want your dog in their laps.

the dog. One must not forget that a Bichon is first and foremost a dog, and that one of the basic needs of all dogs is to have a "pack leader." A pack leader sets boundaries and in so doing gives the members of the pack a sense of security.

Setting and enforcing those boundaries does not intimidate your dog or diminish his spontaneity. Setting limits actually establishes a line of communication between you and your dog that works for both of you.

The problems that Bichon owners may run into are the basic "growing up and learning the rules" situations that dog owners of most any breed face. The Bichon is not particularly destructive or stubborn. If anything, the breed is inclined to be a little bit lazy about rules, ignoring them if they are not consistently enforced.

Chewing: It is important not to confuse your dog. A dog cannot tell the difference between your discarded old slipper and your newest pair of dress shoes. Both smell exactly like you and are just as chewable. Don't expect your dog to understand that it is okay to chew on one and not the other. Never give your dog any of your personal items to chew on; you must help him learn that none of the smell-just-like-you items are playthings.

Dogs chew things because they enjoy doing so. Chewing relieves stress and boredom. Half the battle is in preventing dogs from chewing the wrong things. Don't give your dog the opportunity to do so. Make sure he is confined to his crate or dog-proof room with something okay to chew when you are not there to supervise. Sound cruel? Think again. Which is more cruel, safely confining your dog when you are not there or flying into a rage because the dog entertained himself by eating a hole in the sofa while you were gone?

Housebreaking problems: Housebreaking is based upon a dog's natural dislike for eliminating where it eats and sleeps. Again, supervision is your greatest asset here. A dog does not have to eliminate near its food or sleeping place when given the freedom of the whole house. The housebreaking process is dealt with in detail elsewhere in this book, but this is a reminder of the value of confinement and routine in this respect.

Jumping up: Even people who like dogs do not particularly like to be jumped upon when they enter someone's home. Consistency is the only thing that works here. Do not let your dog jump up on your leg or anyone else's—ever. To your Bichon a leg is a leg, and if it is okay to jump up on your leg for a pat, then in his mind all other legs are fair game as well.

When your Bichon runs joyfully to greet you and jumps up for a pat, give the command *"Off!"* and push his paws off your leg. Just as soon as his paws hit the floor, praise him lavishly. Everyone in the family must do this or it will not work. When you and your dog are away from home, have him under control on his leash and repeat the command when he attempts to jump up on strangers.

Fear of being alone: Dogs are social creatures, and some become more upset at being left alone than others do. They may bark, whine, or attempt to destroy things. All dogs must learn that your absence is simply a matter of routine. Don't treat your departure or return like the climax in a romance novel. Dogs get caught up in your emotional responses. If your dog relates your coming and going with hugging, kissing, and all kinds of heightened emotion, it upsets his dependent nature and creates anxiety.

Feeling secure in the kennel or cage you have provided is the first step in your Bichon's "home alone" training. This nips any chance of destructive behavior in the bud. Going in and out of the room while he is confined is the next stage. He is learning that you do come back.

The Bichon is an all-weather dog but avoid extremes. The breed especially dislikes bright sun and high temperatures.

Dogs like to chew and at times it helps them relieve stress or boredom. However, it is up to you to decide what your Bichon can and cannot chew.

All dogs love to dig and the Bichon is no exception. In the proper place no harm can be done, but bathing and re-grooming usually follow a digging episode.

lie in. Perhaps the Bichon's ancient ancester, the Barbet water dog, makes the breed particularly fond of dirt, mud, and water, but whatever the reason, like it they do. Correcting the digging problem is not easy.

Again, supervision works best. If it is not possible to supervise your dog while he is outdoors, keep him in until you can be there to watch what is going on. The minute he attempts to dig, let him know with that tried and true *"No!"* command that this is not acceptable. Good luck on this one!

Spaying and Neutering

All companion Bichons, whether male or female, should be sexually altered unless specifically purchased to breed or to show. Only a Bichon purchased from a breeder who has recommended that it be bred should be allowed to have offspring. You would be astounded by how many dogs and cats, numbering in the millions, are put to sleep each year because they have no homes.

I trust that you, as a responsible dog owner would never allow your Bichon to roam the streets, nor would you consider turning him over to the dog pound. Yet there is no way you can guarantee that someone who might purchase a puppy from you will not be irresponsible and permit the dog to roam or wind up being euthanized at the pound.

Parents who wish to have their young children "experience the miracle of birth" can do

Stepping outside the house but remaining within earshot comes next. The minute the barking or howling begins, you must command *"No!"* Increase the time you are out of sight but not out of earshot. Eventually your absence will go by unnoticed. This may take longer to accomplish with some dogs than it does with others, but persistence is the key. When being left alone is no longer a traumatic experience, you can experiment with leaving your dog loose in a room or in the house if you wish, but again, this should be done gradually. However, the best and safest place for your dog when you are away is in his crate.

Digging: Dogs like to dig. They do it to relieve boredom and to find a nice cool spot to

Remember, spaying the female and neutering the male should be taken care of as early as your veterinarian thinks it is practical.

so by renting videos of animals giving birth. Handling the experience this way saves adding to the serious pet overpopulation.

There is constant lobbying throughout America to restrict the rights of all dog owners and dog breeders because of this pet overpopulation and the unending need to destroy unwanted animals. Thoughtful dog owners will leave the breeding process to experienced individuals who have the facilities to keep all resulting offspring on their premises until suitable and responsible homes can be found for them.

Altering your pet can also avoid some of the more distasteful aspects of dog ownership. As previously discussed, males that have not been altered have the natural instinct to lift their legs and urinate on objects to mark the territory in which they live. It is extremely difficult to teach an unaltered male not to do this in your home.

Female Bichons that have not been spayed will have two estrus cycles a year that are accompanied by a bloody discharge. Unless the female is kept confined, there will be extensive soiling of the area in which she is allowed.

Good Behavior

Responsible owners will have begun training when their Bichon arrived. Trying to undo bad habits is extremely difficult for the trainer and very bewildering for a dog. For instance, a dog that has been permitted to sleep on its owner's bed or climb up on furniture for many months simply cannot understand why, starting today, this is no longer allowable. You may well have a good reason for making this change, but you will be hard pressed to make your Bichon understand the reason. What will result instead is a constant war; your Bichon will do everything in his power to resume his comfortable habit, and you will lose patience with his attempts to do so.

If your Bichon's first attempts to break any household rule is met with a sharp "No!" it is highly unlikely the issue will become a contest of wills. I cannot emphasize enough the value of avoiding rather than correcting bad habits.

The Sit and Stay Commands

First, it is important to remember that the Bichon-in-training should be on collar and leash for this and all other lessons. This will make it impossible for your Bichon to try to dash off to avoid having to do something it might not want to do at that moment.

Give the *Sit* command immediately before pushing down on your Bichon's hindquarters. Praise him lavishly when he does sit, even though you were the one who made the action take place. A food treat always seems to get the lesson across to your canine student more quickly.

Continue holding your Bichon's rear end down, repeating the *Sit* command several times. If he makes an attempt to get up, repeat the command again while exerting pressure on the rear end until the correct position is main-

Give the "sit" command just before you push down on your bichon's hindquarters.

tained. Make your Bichon stay in this position for increasing lengths of time. Begin with a few seconds and increase the time as lessons progress over the following weeks.

Any attempt to get up or to lie down should be corrected by saying, *"No, sit!"* in a firm voice. This should be accompanied by returning him to the desired sit position. Only when you decide your dog should get up should he be allowed to do so. When you do decide he can get up, call his name, say, *"Okay"* and make a big fuss over him. Praise and a food treat are in order every time your dog responds correctly.

Once the *sit* lesson has been mastered, you may start on the *stay* command. With your dog on leash and facing you, command him to sit. Take a step or two back. If he attempts to follow you, say firmly, *"Sit, stay!"* At the same time raise your hand, palm toward him, and again command, *"Stay!"*

Any attempt on your dog's part to get up must be corrected immediately, returning him to the sit position and repeating, *"Stay!"* Once your Bichon begins to understand what he must do, you can gradually increase the distance you step back from a few steps to a few yards. Your Bichon eventually must learn that the

sit, stay commands must be obeyed no matter how far away you are. Later on, with advanced training, your Bichon will learn that the command must be obeyed even when you move entirely out of sight.

When your Bichon begins to understand what you wish in this lesson and has remained in the sit position for as long as you have dictated, do not make the mistake of calling him to you at first. This makes him overly anxious to get up and run to you. Instead, walk back to the dog and repeat, *"Okay"* a signal that the command is over. Later, when it becomes more reliable in this respect, you can call him to you.

The *sit, stay* lesson can take considerable time and patience. We reserve at least the *stay* part of the training until the Bichon is at least six months old, because everything in a very young Bichon puppy's makeup dictates that, for protection, he get up and follow you wherever you go. Forcing a very young puppy to operate against his natural preservation instincts can be bewildering.

The Lie Down Command

Once your Bichon has mastered the *sit* and *stay* commands, you may begin work on *lie down*. This is especially useful if you want your

OBEDIENCE TRAINING

Bichon to remain in a particular place for a long period of time.

Early in the training there can be a little more resistance to obeying the *lie down* command than there was to the *sit* command. Once dogs have become accustomed to lying down on command, it seems to be more relaxing for them and they seem less apt to want to get up and wander.

With you kneeling and your Bichon sitting in front of and facing you, give the command, *"Lie down!"* Then reach down and slide his front feet toward you. He will automatically then be lying down. Again, praise and a food treat are appropriate. Continue helping your Bichon into the *"Lie down"* position until he does so on his own. Be firm and be patient. Obeying this command can take a bit of time before some dogs respond, even when they understand fully what you want them to do.

Avoid Confusion

Don't confuse your Bichon by using the same command for different things. For instance, you have been using the *off* command to have him get off the sofa or stop jumping up on your leg. You are teaching him that *lie down* means stretching out on the floor. Don't say *"down"* when you want your Bichon off the sofa or off your leg. Although the difference is very clear to you, it does nothing but confuse your dog.

The Heel Command

Teaching your Bichon to heel is the very basis for future off-leash control. In learning to *heel*, your dog will walk on your left side with his shoulder next to your leg no matter which direction you might go. We do not advocate ever having your dog off leash when away from home, but it is reassuring to know that your dog will obey and stay with you regardless of circumstances. It should be easy to see how important a lesson this will be for safety's sake.

Once your puppy has learned the "sit" command you can start working on "stay."

A lightweight, link-chain training collar is very useful for the heeling lesson. It provides both quick pressure around the neck and a snapping sound, both of which get the dog's attention. Erroneously referred to as a "choke collar," the link-chain collar used properly will not choke the dog.

As soon as your Bichon has learned to walk along on the leash, insist that he walk on your left side. A quick short jerk on the leash will keep him from lunging from side to side, pulling ahead, or lagging back. Always keep the leash slack while your dog maintains the proper position at your side. Should he begin to drift away, give the *heel* command, followed immediately by a sharp jerk on the leash, and guide him back to the correct position.

Do not pull on the leash with steady pressure. A sharp but gentle jerking motion is what is needed to get your dog's attention. It is amazing how quickly most Bichons learn to obey the *heel* command. This is a breed that is quick to learn and eager to please.

Training Classes

For obedience work beyond the basic lessons required for him to be a good canine citizen it is wise for the Bichon owner to seek out local professional assistance.

FEEDING YOUR BICHON

Your Bichon can be put on an adult feeding schedule at about ten months of age. This means the adult Bichon will receive one main meal a day, preferably at the same time each evening. This meal is supplemented by a morning snack, for this we highly recommend hard dog biscuits. These not only prove to be much anticipated treats, but do wonders toward maintaining healthy gums and teeth.

How Much Food?

The correct amount of food to maintain a Bichon's optimum condition varies as much from dog to dog as it does from human to human. Much depends upon how much your Bichon exercises. A dog that is given a sedate walk once or twice a day and is otherwise confined to a small apartment is going to require less food than a dog that has the freedom to run the entire house and yard. On the other hand, a Bichon that has a rough-and-ready canine companion or one that frolics with young children all day will need considerably more food than the more sedentary dog.

The correct amount of food for a normally active Bichon is that which she will eat readily within about 15 minutes of being given the meal. What your dog does not eat in that

The happy healthy Bichon you bring into your home will stay that way as long as he or she is well cared for nutritionally.

amount of time should be taken up and discarded. Leaving food out for extended periods of time can lead to erratic and finicky eating habits.

Although some breeds of dogs will eat as much as you give them and become obese, this is seldom the case with a Bichon. In our many years of involvement with the breed, we have seen only one or two Bichons that one would consider seriously overweight.

Unfortunately it is not unusual to find the opposite to be true. Some Bichons can become very picky eaters. This is usually brought about by overly solicitous owners who panic at their dog's first refusal of food and begin to hand-feed, or tempt her to eat by offering expensive and often totally non-nutritious treats.

Fresh water and a properly prepared balanced diet containing the essential nutrients in correct proportions is all a healthy dog needs to be offered. If your Bichon will not eat the food offered, it is because she is either not hungry or not well. If the former is the case, she will eat

Regardless of your Bichon's dietary needs, today's dog food manufacturers can supply the kind of dry or canned food required. If not carried in supermarket or pet store, most veterinarians carry specialized food products.

HELPFUL HINT: The better foods are not normally manufactured to look like products that appeal to humans. A dog does not care that a food looks like a sirloin steak or a wedge of cheese. All a dog cares about is how food smells and tastes. The "looks like" dog foods are manufactured to tempt the dog's owner, but because it is highly unlikely that you will be eating your dog's food, do not waste your money.

Be aware of canned or moist products that have the look of "rich red beef" or dry food that is red in color. In most cases the color put there to appeal to you is achieved through the use of red dye. This dye may not be toxic, but dye is dye, and it will stain the hair around your Bichon's mouth.

A good red dye test is to place a small amount of canned or well-moistened dry food on a piece of white paper towel. Let the food sit there for about a half hour and then check to see if the towel has been stained. If the toweling has taken on a red stain, you can rest assured your Bichon's facial hair would do the same.

when she is hungry. If you suspect the latter, an appointment with your veterinarian is in order.

Canned Food or Dry?

A great deal of research is conducted by manufacturers of the leading brands of dog food to determine the exact ratio of vitamins and minerals necessary to maintain your dog's well-being. This applies to both canned and dry foods, but like most other things in life, "you get what you pay for." It costs the manufacturer more to produce a nutritionally balanced, high-quality food that a dog can digest than it does to produce a brand that provides only marginal nourishment.

Dogs, whether Chihuahuas, Great Danes, or Bichons are carnivorous (meat-eating) animals, and although the vegetable content of their diet should not be overlooked, their physiology and anatomy are based upon carnivorous food acquisition. Protein and fat are absolutely essential to a dog's well-being. The animal protein and fat your dog needs can be replaced by some vegetable proteins, but the amounts and the kind require a clear understanding of nutrition.

There are so many excellent commercial dog foods available today that it seems a waste of time, effort, and money to try to duplicate the

To prevent facial hair staining avoid feeding your Bichon Frise foods that contain red dye. Red dye is often added to dog foods to achieve the look of meat.

nutritional content of these carefully thought-out products by cooking food from scratch. It is important, though, that you read labels carefully or consult with your veterinarian, who will help you select the best moist or dry food for your Bichon.

Whether canned or dry, look for a food in which the main ingredient is derived from meat, poultry, or fish. Remember that you cannot purchase a top-quality dog food for the same price as one that lacks the nutritional value you are looking for. In many cases you will find that not only does your Bichon need less of the better food, but there will be less fecal waste as well.

older Bichon gets some moderate exercise each day. The old-timer may prefer to spend most of his day on the sofa or comfortable pillow, but moderate exercise will keep your friend alive much longer.

Special Diets

A good number of dog-food manufacturers now produce special diets for overweight, underweight, and aged dogs. The calorie content of these foods is adjusted to suit the particular problem that accompanies each condition.

There is no better remedy for these conditions, however, than using good, common sense. Too many calories and too little exercise will increase weight. Fewer calories reduce weight. The adult Bichon that is underweight would probably do well on a diet specially developed for puppies, because it is much higher in caloric content.

The aged dog needs a much lower-calorie diet than the growing puppy or even adult Bichon. It is also important to make sure your

TIP

Check Labels

By law, every container of dog food must list all the ingredients in descending order by weight. The major ingredient is listed first, the next most prominent follows, and so on down the line.

A diet based on meat or poultry (appearing first in the ingredient list) is going to provide more nutrition per pound of food than one that lists a filler grain product as a major ingredient. The diet based on meat and poultry will also cost more than a food heavy in inexpensive fillers.

BATHING AND GROOMING

Most breeders begin to accustom Bichon puppies to being groomed and trimmed as soon as they have enough hair to brush. By the time your puppy is ready to come home with you she undoubtedly will have become used to being held to have her nails trimmed and, her ears cleaned, and to sitting still long enough to have preliminary trimming around the eyes, under the tail, and so forth.

Care of the Puppy Coat

We would certainly question the reliability of the kennel involved if your puppy were not exposed to these preliminary trimming steps by the time she was ready to go home with you. If this should be the case, however, you must begin these grooming lessons immediately. The older a Bichon puppy has grown without learning to accept grooming procedures, the more frightened she will be initially of what you are attempting to do. Regardless of the amount of resistance your Bichon puppy may put up, remember that she is objecting to something that she does not like, not to something that will harm her.

Grooming is a part of every dog's life and is a major factor in keeping your Bichon clean,

Good grooming habits are necessary in order for the breed to maintain that classic "powder puff" look.

healthy, and looking like a Bichon. Begin gently but firmly to accustom the new puppy to these procedures. A few minutes are sufficient at first; gradually increase the length of time.

Do not attempt to accomplish your grooming efforts on the floor. The puppy will only attempt to get away and you will spend half your time chasing the unwilling youngster around the room. Buy or build a small grooming table of a height that allows you to stand or sit comfortably while you work. Adjustable-height grooming tables are available at most pet shops. The size of the top of the grooming table should be just large enough for an adult Bichon to stand or lie down upon, no larger.

Although brushing the Bichon puppy will not take a particularly long time, the situation will be quite different when your Bichon has grown up and developed a mature coat. The two of you are going to spend considerable time at the grooming table, so you might as

The best place to groom your Bichon is on a grooming table made for that purpose. These tables can be purchased at your local pet emporium or they can be built in your home workshop.

well start early to teach your puppy to lie down on the table and enjoy all the attention she is getting. This is also a good time and place to practice the *sit* and *lie down* lessons.

A prominent part of the look of the Bichon Frise as a breed is its "powder puff" coat. This coat type is of course in large part hereditary, but proper grooming procedures keep it looking as it should.

A Bichon puppy's coat is nothing like what it will be when the puppy reaches maturity. Puppy hair is finer, softer, and very wispy if allowed to grow without being cut back (called *tipping*). Tipping simply means you are cutting back your puppy's coat a small amount all over except for the ear fringes, moustache, beard, and tail. These are the areas that require length rather than any amount of texture.

Some time between 9 and 12 months of age you will note that your Bichon's coat will consistently mat and tangle, especially if you have not been diligent in keeping the coat tipped and brushed. At this point you will note that a

thick, soft undercoat is beginning to develop close to the skin, whereas the outer coat is still silky and sparse. This undercoat is what will hold up the adult hair and help create that powder puff look so typical of the Bichon. The appearance of this undercoat tells you your puppy is passing into adolescence and her adult coat is beginning to develop.

It is hoped that you and your puppy have worked out any difficulties you may have had surrounding grooming and trimming, because constant care and brushing during this coat-change period is critical to avoid matting. From now on your Bichon should be brushed at least two or three times a week. Never allow a mat to go unattended. Regular brushing will remove the dead puppy hair before it has a chance to create mats and will encourage the growth of the new hair. Use the pin brush to do this. The slicker brush may be used on the hair of the legs and to separate hair around a mat. If you do use the slicker brush on the body coat or longer hair of the head and tail, do so with extreme care and only by separating the coat into layers and carefully brushing from the root of the hair out, being careful not to pull out undercoat. Never drag the slicker brush over the top of the hair.

Bathing

Preparing for the bath: Never bathe a matted Bichon! Your efforts will only result in more and larger mats. Before bathing, the coat must be brushed out completely and thoroughly with the pin brush. Do not neglect the hard-to-reach areas: between the front legs, under the front legs where they join the body, and between the rear legs. Should you find mats, it is not necessary to cut them out. Sprinkle baby powder or grooming powder made for that purpose into the coat and brush completely from the skin out. Help to separate the mat with your fingers, taking care not to tear the hair loose.

Brushing must be done thoroughly and gently. What is referred to as *line-brushing* is undoubtedly the best method. This method requires your Bichon to be lying down on its side. Starting at the dog's spine and where the hind leg joins the body, part the hair in a straight line down to the abdomen. Take your left hand and hold down the hair on the left side of the part. Brush through the hair to the right of the part that is not held down. You will be brushing to your right.

Next, make another part about 2 inches (5 cm) to the left and parallel to the first part that you made and again brush gently through the hair that is not held down. Proceed on toward the front of the dog, continually repeating the parting process until you reach the head. Then turn your dog over on its other side and repeat the process. This same method can be used on the top of the head, chest, legs, and the longer furnishings as well.

When you are finished, you will have gone over every square inch of the dog and it will be totally free of mats and tangles. When doing the longer hair on the tail and ears, be very

Use a heavy towel to absorb as much bath water as possible out of your freshly bathed dog. This will considerably decrease drying time.

TIP

Bathing Equipment Needed
Rubber mat—to be placed on the bottom of sink or tub to keep your dog from slipping

Rubber spray hose—for thorough wetting and rinsing

Shampoo—especially made for white dogs

Mineral oil or petroleum jelly—a drop or small dab applied directly to each eye to protect the eyes from soap irritation

Cotton balls—one in each ear to protect the inner ear from water

Large towel—bath size to be used for partial drying

Hair dryer—for blow drying the freshly bathed Bichon

CHECKLIST

Necessary Grooming Supplies

Hair dryer—to be used to brush-dry your Bichon immediately after his bath.

Pin brush—for body coat from the time it reaches any considerable length. The pin brush has long, pliable metal bristles or "pins" set in a cushioned rubber base and is ideal for Bichon coats, because it does not pull out the undercoat.

Slicker brush—for puppy coats and shorter coats and for legs and feet of longer-coated dogs. This is an oblong metal brush with a handle. The metal teeth are bent and are set in rubber. This brush should be used sparingly and gently on the adult Bichon's coat, because it will pull out the undercoat you are trying to protect if used without care.

Medium/fine comb—the teeth on this comb (often called a *greyhound comb*) are divided in half, part being set very close together and the other half set wider. This comb is used for beard, head, and tail and to lift body coat while trimming.

Hemostat or tweezers—for removing hair from the inside of the ears, an important part of grooming.

Barber's haircutting shears—specifically designed for haircutting. The better the scissors, the more professional looking the trim job will be.

Nail clippers—designed specifically for trimming your dog's nails.

Grooming table—with a corrugated or rough rubber mat top to keep the dog from slipping. The table must be firm and steady and of a height that permits you to work comfortably.

gentle, as this hair seems to be extremely fragile and easily broken and pulled loose. The only hair that you want to remove is dead hair that has already come loose.

The Bichon's inquisitive nature will undoubtedly result in mini-disasters at one time or another. Gum, tar, and other foreign substances will find their way into your dog's coat, but it is seldom necessary to cut the hair to correct the problem.

There are many home remedies we have used to cope with such accidents, but the best we have found is a lotion called Avon Skin So Soft, which can be purchased at your local drugstore. Saturate the affected area of the coat with the lotion and allow it to penetrate the foreign substance. The lotion will loosen the gum or tar and you will be able to slide it off with little or no damage to the hair. Repeat if necessary, and when the substance has been entirely removed, wash and rinse the area thoroughly or give the dog a complete bath.

Be firm but gentle when placing your Bichon in the tub. Most Bichons will not object to their bath, but there are always those that mistrust anything new or strange and will do their best to avoid having to endure it. Because, this is a breed that will spend a good portion of its life in the tub, cooperation is essential. Again, be firm but gentle.

Learning proper brushing techniques will make your grooming issue easier and more thorough.

Your Bichon should be wet down completely with the rubber spray hose using warm, not hot, water. Shampoo and wash well, using extra shampoo on stained or extra-dirty areas, particularly on the beard, legs, and tail. Read shampoo directions carefully; some are concentrated and need to be diluted before using. Others contain bluing agents and should be left on the dog only for a specific length of time.

When using medicated shampoos, spot test to see if the product stains your Bichon's coat. If the product does stain, check with your groomer or veterinarian to see if there is a substitute product that will not discolor your Bichon's coat.

Start behind the ears and work back, working the lather well into the coat. Then return to the head and carefully shampoo and rinse this area. Dogs, like humans, will react strongly to having soap rubbed into their eyes, nose, or mouth, so wash the head area carefully.

Shampoo should be rinsed out immediately. Repeat the entire process, and this time place special emphasis on final rinsing. You can't rinse too much. Shampoo left in the coat can cause mats and skin irritation.

With the dog still in the tub, squeeze as much water out of the coat as you can. Then wrap your dog in the towel you have nearby

and carry the dog to your grooming table. Here you will towel-dry to remove excess moisture in preparation for brush drying.

Drying

Immediately after a quick towel drying, brush through the damp coat quickly with the pin brush. This will remove any tangles created while bathing or in the preliminary towel drying.

Using the hair dryer and pin brush, you will then commence with the brush-drying process. Set your hair dryer at medium setting. The hot setting may be quicker, but it can dry out the hair shafts, causing them to split. You must also be careful not to burn the skin of your Bichon with a dryer that is too hot.

Brush drying is the only way you can get the Bichon's coat to stand out from the body and achieve the "powder puff" look of the breed. Allowing the Bichon's hair to dry on its own without using a hair dryer and brush will cause the hair to curl up. You will not be able to scis-

HELPFUL HINT: Investing in a dryer that has a stand can be a great help in brush drying. This will allow you to direct the flow of air to where it is needed and free both your hands to attend to brushing.

As your Bichon approaches a year of age there will be an appreciable increase in the amount and density of the coat. It will take more time and effort to keep the coat tangle free.

HELPFUL HINT: The inner ear and nails should be taken care of at this time as well. Once your Bichon is in the tub you can attend to cleaning the anal glands also. Doing so while the dog is in the tub allows you to flush the foul-smelling excretion down the drain immediately. Refer to the section on "Home Health Care" for more details.

brush to do the final drying and straightening. Again, be careful not to pull hair out.

After you have completed the head and neck, follow your line-brushing process with the dog lying on its side. You must be sure to dry and brush thoroughly under the arms and between the legs. Any hair left to dry on its own, especially in the hard-to-get places, is sure to mat.

Once your Bichon is completely dry, you must begin the trimming process immediately. If trimming is delayed, the hair begins to curl and all your brush-drying efforts will have been useless.

Scissoring

The main difference between the pet trim and the correct show trim is primarily in the length of hair, but the details of the show trim are far more complex. The pet trim is much shorter and easier to maintain. The attractive show trim takes a great deal more care to keep up, and the long hair collects leaves and twigs if your Bichon has regular access to the outdoors.

If dog shows are in your Bichon's future, you should ask your breeder for a recommendation or attend a dog show in your area. There will undoubtedly be people there showing their Bichons who will be able to assist you with questions you might have about finding a professional groomer.

sor smoothly to get that plush powder puff look if you allow the hair to curl.

Actually the line-brushing method you used before the bath is the best way to brush-dry as well, except that it is best to begin at the head and neck with the dog lying on its stomach. Point your dryer at the area to be brushed, using light strokes repeatedly until that section is completely dry, then move on to the next section. With each section of damp hair, use the pin brush to make the part and the slicker

Trimming a Bichon Frise for the show ring requires years of practice or the talents of a professional show groomer.

Much later when you become more experienced and have ample opportunity to practice, you may be able to learn to trim your Bichon for the ring yourself. The standard of the breed is very specific about how the Bichon should be groomed for showing, but helpful charts and instruction booklets are available at dog show bookstands and on many online book web sites.

The decision you make about a show career for your Bichon will determine how liberal you can be in regard to your dog's play and exercise. The Bichon coat is relatively sturdy and can handle normal rough-and-tumble play with other dogs. If the other dogs like to chew on your dog's coat, obviously you are going to have a problem. Your dog will still be able to accompany you on walks and hikes, but a roll in wet green grass can easily stain the coat.

Proper Use of the Comb

Learning proper use of the comb while trimming will assist you greatly in achieving the desired results. Constantly lift the hair up and out as you go along. This keeps all the hairs standing directly away from the dog's body, and with practice you will be able to achieve that smooth but plush look you are after.

HELPFUL HINT: It is very important to note that in trimming the head of the Bichon, the objective is to create a rounded look. There should be no indentation where the ears join the head, as you might see in a poodle trim.

Remember that the hair of the beard, ears, and tail is always left much longer than the rest of the coat. The actual length depends upon whether the Bichon is being trimmed for the show ring or as a companion.

TIP

No Shaving!

Only under extreme circumstances (such as the coat's being entirely matted to the skin) should you ever consider shaving your Bichon. The coat serves as insulation against both heat and cold. Misguided owners think they are doing their dog a service by shaving them in the summer, when exactly the opposite is true.

VETERINARY CARE AND INHERITED PROBLEMS

Minor accidents and illnesses as well as problems of a more serious nature will undoubtedly occur while your Bichon progresses through puppyhood, adolescence, and on into old age. This chapter is written in the hope that it will help the Bichon owner determine the difference between situations that can easily be taken care of at home and those that demand veterinary treatment.

When to Call the Veterinarian

One piece of advice always applies: If you are in doubt about the seriousness of your Bichon's problem, do not hesitate to pick up the phone and call your veterinarian. In most cases veterinarians know which questions to ask and will be able to determine whether or not it is necessary to see your dog.

Major Illnesses

Very effective vaccines have been developed to combat diseases that once were fatal to practically any infected dog. The danger of

The veterinarian will prove to be your Bichon's best friend next to you.

your Bichon's being infected with distemper, hepatitis, hard pad, leptospirosis, or the extremely virulent parvovirus is highly unlikely if proper inoculations and booster shots have been given regularly.

Rabies among well-cared-for dogs is practically unheard of, but dogs that come in contact with animals in nature can be at risk if not immunized. On occasion, however, there are dogs that, for one reason or another, do not develop full immunity.

Immunization against these infectious diseases begins in puppyhood, and it is extremely important that you follow your veterinarian's inoculation schedule. Neglecting to do so could easily cost your Bichon's life.

It is important to recognize the early symptoms of these diseases should your dog be one

Your Bichon does not have to be in a kennel environment in order to contract kennel cough (infectious rhinotracheitis). It is similar to a mild case of the flu in humans.

When in Doubt, Call Your Veterinarian

- Persistent coughing or sneezing
- Gasping for breath
- Vomiting
- Diarrhea
- Continued listlessness
- Loss of appetite
- Excessive thirst
- Runny nose
- Discharge from the eyes or ears
- Blood in the stool
- Limping, trembling, or shaking
- Abscesses, lumps, or swellings
- Dark or cloudy urine
- Difficult urination
- Loss of bowel or bladder control
- Gums appear deep red or white

of the unfortunate few that has not developed complete immunity. Any marked change in your dog's behavior should be observed very closely. This is especially so if your dog is less than a year old.

Should your Bichon suddenly become listless, refuse food, and start to cough and sneeze, contact your veterinarian at once. Other signs of possible problems in this area are marked increase in thirst, blood in the stools or urine, and discharge of any kind from the nose.

Accidents

Injuries sustained in a road accident can be fatal if not handled correctly and promptly. If your Bichon is struck by an automobile or motorcycle, it is important that you remain calm. Panic on your part will serve only to upset the injured animal and could cause him to thrash about and injure himself even more seriously.

If your Bichon is unable to move on his own, immediately remove him from the street where he could be injured further. In picking up your injured dog it is critical that you support his body as fully as possible. The less movement of the injured area the better. Do not wait to determine the extent of injury. Internal injuries may have occurred that you are unable to observe immediately. Get the injured dog to a veterinarian without delay. Ask someone to drive you there so that you are free to hold your injured dog and keep him calm. If no one else is available to drive you, put your injured dog in a container of some kind to keep him as immobile as possible.

Bleeding Wounds

If there is a bleeding wound caused by a traffic accident or any other accident, deal with the bleeding at once. Using a pad of cotton or a compress soaked in cold water, apply pressure directly to the bleeding point. If the flow of blood is not stemmed, your dog could bleed to death.

Bichons seldom pick fights with other dogs, but their friendly attitude can spark hostility on the part of other, more aggressive dogs. Should your Bichon be attacked by another dog, get the two dogs apart as quickly as you can and get your dog to the veterinarian without delay. Bite wounds are invariably infected, and antibiotic treatment is necessary.

Kennel Cough

Kennel cough (infectious rhinotracheitis), although highly infectious, is not a serious disease. It is like a mild case of influenza in humans. A mixture of bacteria and a virus causes kennel cough. The name of the disease is misleading in that it implies that a dog must be in a kennel environment to be infected. Actually it is very easily passed from one dog to another in almost any situation.

The symptoms can make the disease sound far worse than it actually is. It is charaterized by a persistent hacking cough that at times makes one think that surely the dog will bring up everything he has ever eaten!

Various protective procedures are available that can be administered by your veterinarian. In addition to inoculations, there is an intranasal vaccine.

Bladder Stones

Bladder stones (urolithiasis) and bladder infections are one of the major health problems

When an accident occurs it is imperative to lift your dog with as much support to the body as possible.

in the Bichon Frise. There are two types of these stones: struvite and calcium oxalate. The former is caused by infection and is not considered to be inherited. Calcium oxalate stones, on the other hand, are inherited. Complicating the situation is that the calcium oxate stones can eventually have a coating of struvite if not properly treated and thereby cause a misdiagnosis.

Bladder stones form when excess minerals and other waste products crystallize in the bladder. Symptoms are frequent urination, blood in the urine, general weakness, and loss of appetite. Immediate veterinary care must be

Life cycle of the tapeworm: fleas are commonly hosts of the tapeworm. When the flea is swallowed the parasite is shared with your dog, tapeworms develop and segments are passed in the feces.

sought if any of these symptoms is observed, because untreated the condition can cause severe and permanent kidney damage and even death in extreme cases.

Internal Parasites

Tapeworms and heartworms are best diagnosed and treated by your veterinarian. Great advances are continually being made in dealing with both these parasites and what was once a complicated and time-consuming treatment has been simplified over the years.

Tapeworms: Tapeworms are a part of the life cycle of the flea. If your Bichon has or has had fleas, she undoubtedly has tapeworm. A sign

of infection is the appearance of segments of the worm crawling around the dog's anus or in the stool just after the dog has relieved itself. Your veterinarian can inoculate your Bichon if he has this problem, and the tapeworms are quickly and completely eliminated.

Roundworms: Roundworms are not an unusual condition in dogs and are rarely harmful in an adult dog. However, these parasites can cause extreme health hazards to puppies if present in large amounts.

Roundworms can be transmitted from mother to puppies. It is wise to make sure that your female is free of roundworms before you breed her should you ever plan on a litter of puppies.

Heartworms: Heartworms are parasitic worms found in dogs' hearts. Dogs are the only mammals that are commonly affected. The worm is transmitted by mosquitoes that carry the larvae of the worm.

Your veterinarian can detect the presence of heartworm by a blood test.

There are preventive medications for a dog that tests negative and corrective measures for the dog that has been infected.

Stings and Bites

Bichons are curious little animals and seem fascinated by all things that fly and crawl. Naturally they attempt to examine insects with their paws or mouths. This can lead to bites and stings on the foot, or worse, on or around the mouth or nose.

If the sting is visible, remove it with a pair of tweezers and apply a saline solution or mild antiseptic. If the swelling is large, particularly inside the mouth, or if the dog appears to be in shock, contact your veterinarian at once.

Foreign Objects

If you see your Bichon pawing at his mouth or rubbing his mouth along the ground, immediately check to see if something is lodged inside. Bichons can be intrigued by small playthings or bones and will chew and worry them until they somehow manage to get the object lodged or trapped across their teeth, usually halfway back or even at the back of the mouth where the two jaws hinge.

Should this be the case, grasp the object firmly between your fingers and push firmly toward the back of the mouth where the teeth are wider. This will usually dislodge the object, but be sure to have a firm grip on the object so the dog does not swallow it. If you are unable to remove the object quickly, get your Bichon to the veterinarian at once.

If you suspect your Bichon has swallowed a small ball or some other object, check to see if the object is visible in his throat. If so, reach in, grasp the object firmly and pull it out. If the dog seems to be experiencing difficulty in breathing, the object may be lodged in the windpipe. Sharp blows to the rib cage may cause him to expel air from the lungs and also expel the object.

If any small object is missing in the home and you suspect your Bichon may have ingested it, do not hesitate to consult your veterinarian. An X ray will reveal the hidden "treasure" and save your dog's life.

Inherited Problems and Diseases

Like all breeds of domesticated dogs, the Bichon Frise has its share of hereditary problems. Probably the only dogs that do not have inherited problems, or at least do not have incapacitating problems, are wild dogs such

CHECKLIST

What You Can Do if Your Bichon Is Poisoned

1. Keep the telephone number of your local poison control center with your other emergency numbers.

2. If you know or suspect which poison your dog has ingested, give this information to the poison control center when you call them. They may be able to prescribe an immediate antidote.

3. Have the emergency number of your dog's veterinarian or the nearest 24-hour emergency veterinary hospital current and easily available. Give any information you receive from the poison control center to your veterinarian.

4. If you are not sure that your dog has been poisoned or which poison he may have ingested, describe the symptoms you are observing to your veterinarian.

5. Common symptoms of poisoning: convulsions, paralysis, tremors, vomiting, diarrhea, stomach cramps, and pains accompanied by whimpering or howling, heavy breathing.

as the dingo of Australia and the wild dog of Africa.

The major reason that wild dogs do not experience the inherited problems of their domesticated cousins is natural selection. Any genetically transferred infirmity that would interfere with the wild dog's ability to nurse as a puppy, to capture food as an adult, or to escape from a predator would automatically eliminate the individual from the gene pool.

We who control the breeding of our domesticated dogs are intent upon saving all the puppies in a litter. In preserving life we also perpetuate health problems. Our humanitarian proclivities have a downside as well.

The Bichon Frise Club of America has an ongoing committee dedicated to determining genetic disorders in the breed. Both the club and experienced breeders have literature available about the following breed problems and how to deal with them.

The diseases described here may not be present in the Bichon you buy nor are these problems necessarily to be found in your Bichon's immediate ancestors. They are breed problems, however, that should be discussed with the breeder from whom you purchase your dog. As noted previously in "Choosing Your Bichon,"

the reputable Bichon breeder is aware of the breed's problems and should be more than willing to discuss them with you.

Orthopedic Diseases

Patella luxation: This condition is also commonly referred to as *slipping stifles*. It is an abnormality of the stifle or knee joint leading to dislocation of the kneecap (patella). Normally the kneecap is in a groove at the lower end of the thighbone. It is held in this position by strong elastic ligaments. If the groove is insufficiently developed, the kneecap will leave its normal position and "slip" to one side or the other of the track in which it is normally held.

The dog may exhibit an intermittent but persistent limp or have difficulty straightening out the knee. In some cases the dog may experience pain. Treatment may require surgery.

Hip dysplasia: This is a developmental disease of the hip joint. The result is instability of the hip joint caused by abnormal contours of one or both of the hip joints. Some dogs might show tenderness in the hip, walk with a limp or swaying gait, or experience difficulty when getting up. Symptoms vary from mild, temporary lameness to severe crippling in extreme cases. The light-bodied Bichon is seldom as severely afflicted as some of the heavier-bodied breeds. Treatment may require surgery.

To determine if the parents of the Bichon you purchase have been screened for orthopedic problems, look for the Orthopedic Foundation for Animals (OFA) number on your dog's AKC registration certificate. This number indicates

Early detection of major illnesses could save your Bichon's life. Listlessness and refusing food should not be overlooked.

If a flea problem presents itself, it is important that all areas indoor and out are treated while the dog is away having a professional flea bath.

that the parents have been screened and registered with the OFA. You can determine which conditions were actually screened for on the foundation's web site (www.offa.org).

Eye Problems

Cataracts: This condition is a loss of the normal transparency of the lens of the eye. One or both eyes may be affected and can involve the lens partially or completely.

Some cataracts occur between the ages of one to six years and are not visible to the naked eye. These are known as *juvenile cataracts*. Senile cataracts occur later in life. In cases where cataracts are complete and affect both eyes, blindness results.

Corneal dystrophy: This is a condition in which there appears to be a spot (or spots) on the surface of the eye. These usually do not affect the dog's eyesight.

Progressive retinal atrophy: This condition, commonly referred to as PRA, is a degenerative disease of the retinal cells of the eye that progresses to blindness. It usually occurs later in a Bichon's life—beyond the age of six years.

Discuss the possibility of these eye problems with the breeder from whom you plan to pur-

chase your Bichon. That person can tell you what tests they have had done on their breeding stock and give you advice on the kinds of tests you should have done if necessary.

Extensive clinical studies sponsored by the Bichon Frise Club of America continue to be done on the inherited nature of these and many other diseases. In the case of both cataracts and PRA, science has substantiated that the problems are inherited as simple recessives.

Immotile Ciliary Dyskinesia

This is a defect in the microscopic hairlike structures found in various parts of the body such as the respiratory tract, uterus, testicles, and eustachian tube of the ear. This defect can cause chronic respiratory infections, sterility in both males and females, and loss of hearing.

It is important to establish a weekly health care routine for your Bichon. Maintaining this schedule will prevent escalation of serious problems that may take expensive veterinary attention.

Eye Care

If the eyes are inflamed or discharging any kind of matter, check for foreign bodies such as soot or weed seeds. Regular flushing of the eye with cotton and cool water will help relieve the eye of debris and pollen. However, secretion of tears and unsightly staining under the eyes can be a problem with white dogs. Have your veterinarian inspect your Bichon's eyes for a condition called *entropion*—a condition in which the eyelid is inverted and the eyelashes cause irritation to the eye. This can be corrected by surgery.

If entropion is not the problem, bathe the eyes frequently and treat the stain by rubbing a product called fuller's earth or cornstarch into the stained hair while it is still wet. After it has dried, the fuller's earth should be very

Starting early with a regular regimen of grooming and health checks are what help keep your Bichon happy and healthy and will avoid serious problems occurring.

carefully brushed out. You can repeat this treatment regularly until the staining has been minimized.

Often even careful veterinary checkups rule out everything that is thought might cause the excess tearing and staining. Still the brown staining exists. Tetracycline has provided an answer for some because it seems to control the tears that stain the face. Talk to your veterinarian about the possibility of a three-to-four-week course of tetracycline. This treatment should not begin until your Bichon's permanent teeth have come in to avoid damage to the developing teeth.

Ear Cleaning

The ears should always be clean and pink. Excess hair inside the ear can create an accumulation of wax and dirt in the ear canal. This excess hair can be easily and quickly removed. Grasp a few hairs at a time with tweezers or a hemostat, with a quick, sharp twist and pull

Nothing other than a cotton swab should ever be used to clean your Bichon's ears.

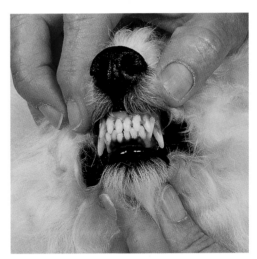

Keep your Bichon's teeth white and clean by thorough and frequent brushing.

they will very easily discharge. Never attempt to cut hair inside the ear canal with scissors or any sharp object.

Nothing other than a cotton swab should ever be inserted into the ear itself—and you should never probe the inner recess of the ear. Moisten the swab with olive or almond oil to clean the ear. If wax has accumulated, dip the swab into rubbing alcohol, squeeze out the excess thoroughly, and clean out the ear.

Do not attempt to treat the ear that has an unpleasant odor. Consult your veterinarian immediately.

Anal Glands

The anal glands are on each side of the anus and should be regularly looked after. They can become blocked, causing extreme irritation and abscesses in advanced cases.

If you notice your Bichon pulling himself along the ground when he is sitting down, you should check the anal glands. It is not a particularly pleasant part of keeping your Bichon

healthy, but if regularly attended to, keeping the anal glands clear is relatively easy.

The best time to attend to this job is when you are giving your Bichon his bath. When he is in the tub, place your thumb and forefinger on either side of the anal passage and exert pressure. The glands will empty quickly. Should you be unsure of how to perform this procedure, your veterinarian, groomer, or the breeder from whom you purchased your Bichon will instruct you.

Dental Care

Care should always be given to the state of your Bichon's teeth. If your Bichon has been accustomed to chewing hard dog biscuits or gnawing on large knuckle or rawhide bones since puppyhood, it is unlikely that you will have any problems. This chewing activity assists greatly in removing dental plaque, which is the major cause of tooth decay. Any sign of redness or decay merits expert attention.

Some Bichons simply do not like to chew. Should this be the case, brushing the teeth at least once a week with a good canine toothpaste will be an important part of your routine. (Do not use toothpaste designed for human use on your dog, because most contain sugar and will cause more harm than good.) This procedure should also be accompanied by regular veterinary checkups.

Retention of baby teeth can cause long-term problems with the permanent teeth. Generally, by the time the permanent teeth have come through at about six or seven months of age, the baby teeth have all fallen out. If there are any baby teeth remaining at this stage, seek your veterinarian's advice on their removal. Retaining baby teeth can interfere with the proper placement of your Bichon's permanent teeth.

Nails

The nails of a dog that spends most of her time indoors or on grass when outdoors can grow long very quickly. Canine nail clippers are available at most pet supply shops. It is best to learn how to use these devices from your veterinarian, groomer, or the breeder from whom you purchased your Bichon before you attempt to use them yourself.

Each nail has a blood vessel running through the center called the quick. Cutting into the quick can be extremely painful to the dog, because it contains very sensitive nerve endings. Severing the quick can also result in a great deal of bleeding that can be difficult to stop. The quick can be seen in light-colored nails, but black nails make it difficult if not impossible to

The nails of most dogs kept in the home will need regular clipping. There are devices available at your pet shop that facilitate performing this task correctly.

determine where the quick ends. When trimming the nails, especially the dark-colored nails, remove only a small portion of the nail at a time. Any number of blood-clotting products, available at pet shops, will almost immediately stem the flow of blood should you cut into the quick.

The quick continues to grow as the nail grows. Cutting near the quick causes it to recede somewhat. Therefore regular trimming will keep the quick well back from the end of the nail. You will find that the quick in neglected nails is very long and comes close to the end of the nail, making it nearly impossible to keep the length of the nail in check. You should seek professional assistance from your veterinarian or groomer to rectify this situation.

Parasites

Fleas: Although fleas are a problem everywhere and for all breeds of dogs, these pests can

Thorough and regular brushing your Bichon Frise will keep you ahead of any parasites that might occur. Even a single flea observed means others lurk on your dog and throughout the household.

be especially troublesome for your Bichon. In fact, some Bichons are highly allergic to fleas, and the very first flea bite can set off a chain of events that can lead to what are commonly referred to as hot spots. They are caused by dog's

chewing and scratching so hard that the skin is broken. If not attended to properly, the areas in which the skin has been broken begin to form moist, painful abscesses, all hair falls away, and a veterinarian must be called upon.

As fastidious as you might be about caring for your Bichon and keeping her coat in good condition, you should realize that fleas will still be a problem. Even your Bichon's daily walks can bring fleas into your home, and once there, the little creatures multiply with alarming rapidity. If you have a cat with access to the outdoors, allowing the cat in and attempting to keep the fleas out will be next to impossible. Those who live in climates in which winter temperatures drop to the freezing point will have a respite from the flea problem, but the rest of the country will battle fleas year-round.

Bathing your Bichon with a good flea soap or product manufactured to eliminate fleas is not enough. If you find fleas—even one flea—on your dog, there are undoubtedly hundreds of others lurking in the carpeting and furniture just waiting for your Bichon to emerge from the tub so that they can hop back on.

The only way to combat fleas is to rid dog, house, and yard of the problem all at the same time. Simultaneously with your Bichon's flea bath you must eliminate fleas from within your home and surrounding outdoor premises.

Flea bombs manufactured for this purpose are available at most hardware stores and veterinary offices. If your Bichon never leaves the

TIP

Tick Removal

To remove adult ticks, soak them with a spray made especially for tick removal; once the parasite has loosened its grip, you can remove it with a pair of tweezers. Regular bathing with a tick dip will prevent reinfestation. But as is the case with all dips and sprays, read the instructions carefully, as some of these products may also be toxic.

confines of your home, which is highly unlikely, using these bombs can help correct the problem. If your Bichon, like most dogs, spends any time at all in your yard or garden, you must simultaneously spray that area with a malathion or diazanon-type spray.

The best method we have found to keep the flea problem in check is for your Bichon to have a flea bath at the dog-grooming salon. Arrange to have a commercial pest control service come to your home while your dog is at the groomer. The service will spray both the interior of your home and the surrounding property. Most of these companies guarantee their work for a specific period of time, and many offer a monthly or quarterly plan by which they will return to make sure the problem does not get out of hand again.

There is always the possibility of toxicity when using flea sprays or flea collars. It is important to read instructions on the packaging of these items very carefully.

Fleas act as carriers of the tapeworm eggs. When a dog swallows a flea, the tapeworm eggs grow in the dog's intestines. The tapeworm is dealt with in the section called "Internal Parasites" in the chapter titled "Veterinary Care and Inherited Problems."

Lice: If no fleas are present and you suspect lice, the dog must be bathed with an insecticidal shampoo every week until the problem is eliminated. Fortunately lice live and breed entirely on the dog, so it is not necessary to treat the entire area in which the dog lives.

Ticks: Your Bichon can pick up ticks by running through grass, wooded areas, or even through sand at the beach. Ticks are bloodsucking insects that bury their heads firmly into the dog's skin. The tick can become a source of extreme

TIP

Common Ailments

The most common canine ailments seem to be vomiting and diarrhea. They do not mean your dog is seriously ill, but should either symptom persist, do not hesitate to call your veterinarian. Dogs may vomit to purge their digestive tracts. Puppies may do so when they overeat or eat too much or too fast. Nervousness or fright can induce vomiting. None of this is cause for alarm unless it occurs repeatedly.

For occasional diarrhea, change from your dog's regular diet to thoroughly cooked rice with a small amount of boiled chicken added. Maintain this kind of diet until the condition improves and then gradually return your dog to its normal diet.

irritation to your dog and can cause secondary infections as well. It is important to have the tick loosen its grip before you attempt to remove it. Otherwise the head may break away from the tick and remain lodged in the dog's skin, which also can create severe infections.

The entire environment in which your Bichon lives must be regularly and vigorously treated against ticks, especially if you live adjacent to a wooded area or grassland. Ticks can transmit serious diseases that can endanger humans as well as animals. Ticks in some areas carry Lyme disease and Rocky Mountain spotted fever. It is important that you discuss the tick problem with your local veterinarian, who can advise you on which dangers might present themselves.

YOU AND YOUR ADULT BICHON

At first thought, having your Bichon accompany you on an extended trip may sound like great fun for both of you. Further consideration could well alter your decision.

Traveling with Your Bichon

One of the first things you must ask yourself is where your Bichon will stay when you stop along the way to eat or to sleep. Unlike most European countries, restaurants in America don't permit dogs to accompany their owners inside. Leaving your dog in a parked automobile while you eat can be very dangerous, as weather conditions can change rapidly and temperatures in a closed car can soar.

Leaving the windows open puts your pet in danger of escaping or being stolen, even if he is safely secured in a traveling container. A slightly open window is of little help once the sun begins to beat down on the car.

Many hotels and motels do not allow dogs into the rooms because other guests have

The adult Bichon has his special needs as well.

abused this privilege in the past. Many accommodations that do allow pets into the rooms charge an extra fee or security deposit. These establishments assume that your dog is accustomed to being left alone in a strange place and will not disturb other guests by barking and howling while you are out of your room.

Also, changing your Bichon's accustomed food and water can create a number of problems, including diarrhea. The latter is not something most people wish to cope with while traveling.

When You Do Travel Together

It should be easy to see that taking your Bichon along with you on a trip will require a good deal of advance planning. An air-conditioned car can help considerably if your trip will be made through areas where daytime temperatures are high. Take the crate or cage that you have been using at home as well.

There are always exercise stops that must be taken along the way when traveling. Be sure to bring brush and comb should those stops find that your Bichon's coat has attracted burrs or debris.

This keeps your pet safe while traveling and provides a safe, secure, and familiar place if you are out of your hotel room.

Stops along the way must be carefully planned. Realize that your selection of restaurants will have to be made with your pet's safety in mind. Your car must not be left in the sun at any stop. Further, unless the weather is very cool, windows should be left open and only when your car can be left where you or a member of your party can see it at all times.

Many people who travel with their pets make an early-morning stop at a grocery store or carryout restaurant and purchase their own food for the day. Meal stops can then be made at some shady spot along the way. Should you decide to do this, it will give you an opportunity to exercise your dog at the same time.

Dinnertime should come after you have checked into your hotel or motel and put your dog in your room. Reservations must be made in advance with those places allowing dogs in the rooms. If you have taken our previous advice and trained your Bichon to stay alone in his kennel or cage, a good part of your problem will be solved. You will not have to worry about barking and howling while you are gone, nor will you run the risk of having your dog cause any damage to the room.

If you have not accustomed your dog to being left alone in his kennel, it is to be hoped that he has at least learned to be left alone. If so, we seriously advise closing your Bichon in the bathroom while you are out of the room. It is also wise to leave a Do Not Disturb sign on your door while you are gone to avoid a staff person's entering your room and allowing your dog to escape.

If your dog will not stay alone in a strange room without barking, do not leave him alone! He can become frenzied and destroy things or disturb the other occupants of the hotel. You must be considerate of others—both people who are not particularly dog-tolerant and those who might wish to stay at the same hotel later with their own dogs. The management of the hotel will not be disposed to allow other people with dogs to stay if you have abused your privileges.

You must take along an adequate supply of your Bichon's accustomed food and water. Changing diets and water can seriously upset your dog, and diarrhea and vomiting are the last things you will want to deal with on your trip.

Do take a brush, comb, and scissors. If you plan to hike or walk your dog along the side of the road, these accessories will enable you to get rid of any unwanted weeds, seeds, or dirt your Bichon's coat might have attracted.

The Senior Citizen

Bichons age remarkably well, and though life spans vary from dog to dog, it is not unusual to find many members of this breed alive and well even at 12 to 14 years of age. Some of these same old-timers have maintained their sight and hearing and all their teeth until their final days!

Exercise

Certain precautions must be taken with the aged Bichon to keep him happy and healthy. Exercise must be adjusted as your Bichon gets older, and you must take pains to see that he is not pushed beyond his capacity when hiking or playing. This is especially so if there are any signs of arthritis and if exercise makes the old fellow limp.

Diet

Your Bichon's diet must also be adjusted accordingly so that there is less strain on the digestive system. The fat content of the food must be reduced. Today most major dog food manufacturers take canine aging into consideration and offer diets specifically geared to the senior citizen.

If your Bichon has been accustomed to one major meal each day, it is probably wise to adjust this to two smaller meals. It is also absolutely necessary to avoid letting the aging dog become overweight. The strain of additional weight will certainly shorten his life span.

Health Problems

Aging frequently affects the Bichon's ability to hear and see. If you find your previously obedient Bichon failing to respond quickly or not at all to your call, make concessions for age.

Also the old Bichon's patience may wear thin much more quickly than it did when he was a youngster. Puppies and children can prove extremely tiresome to the elderly Bichon, and it is up to the owner not to allow the old-timer to be subjected to youthful harassment.

It is not uncommon for some older Bichons to develop diabetes and kidney stones. These conditions are treatable by your veterinarian. Diabetes requires insulin injections on a daily basis. A veterinarian can show you how to administer these inoculations.

Excessive drinking of water can be a sign that the kidneys are not working properly. In some cases this can also be a sign that bitches that have not been spayed are developing pyometra, an inflammation of the womb that requires prompt professional treatment.

Veterinary science has developed many new methods that help your dog stay healthy even through his final years. Regular checkups will prevent rapid progress of the ailments that could lead to your pet's deterioration.

The Last Good-bye

There will come a time, when your canine friend of many years is no longer able to enjoy life and you must make a heart-wrenching decision. Fortunately when science is no longer able to prevent our canine friends' suffering or incontinence, we are able to mercifully bring their lives to a close.

Your veterinarian will tell you when the time has come to do this and will be able to perform this final act with tenderness and skill. Done professionally, there is no stress to your dog, especially if you are there to hold the dog while the veterinarian administers the injection.

This is never an easy decision to make, but carefully considered, it is the kindest action you can take for your canine friend that has given you so many years of companionship and enjoyment.

GROUP
FIRST

THE
WESTMINSTER
KENNEL CLUB
FEBUARY 8 & 9, 1993

NO BUSINESS LIKE SHOW BUSINESS

In addition to providing years of fun and companionship in and around your home, there is another aspect of owning a purebred dog that you may not have considered. The Bichon Frise is a very popular show dog. Many owners who had thought of their Bichon only as a friend and companion have entered the dog show world and found it to be an exciting and fascinating hobby. Dog shows also give competitors an opportunity to create new friendships from all walks of life and are an activity in which the entire family can participate.

Competitive Events

The American Kennel Club sponsors many kinds of competitive events in which all registered purebred dogs may compete: conformation judging, obedience trials, agility trials, field trials, and the more recent Canine Good Citizen events.

Conformation Shows: Currently the most popular and well-attended dog events are conformation shows and obedience trials. The original purpose of conformation shows was to give breeders a means of comparing their stock with that of other fanciers and thereby make improvements in their breeding programs.

The Bichon Frise excels in both brains and beauty.

Today, not all people who participate in conformation shows intend to become breeders. Many simply find enjoyment in the competitive aspect of these events. Referred to by some as "canine beauty contests," conformation dog shows take place nearly every weekend of the year in one part of the country or another and are open to all non-neutered, AKC-registered dogs.

Generally speaking, conformation shows fall into two major categories: matches and championship events. Match shows are primarily staged for young or inexperienced dogs that are not ready to compete for championship points. In most cases classes are offered for dogs from about three months of age and older.

The sparkling white coat contrasting with the black eyes and pigment of the Bichon Frise makes the breed a standout in the show ring.

Match Shows

Matches are an excellent place for novice handlers to learn to show their own dogs. Because these match shows are far more informal than championship events, there is plenty of time for the novice handler to ask questions and seek assistance from more experienced exhibitors or from the officiating judges.

Match shows can be held for all breeds of dogs recognized by the AKC or they can be what are referred to as specialty matches. The latter are for one particular breed of dog. A club devoted to a specific breed in an area will often hold these match shows so that newer club members and young puppies will have an opportunity to gain some experience.

Information about these matches can usually be found in the classified sections of Sunday newspapers under "Dogs for Sale." Local breeders are usually aware of upcoming events of this kind as well.

There is no need to enter these informal matches ahead of time. Most accept entries on the grounds of the show site the morning of the event. The person taking your entry will be able to help you fill out the entry form and give you the preliminary instructions you need.

Championship Shows

Championship shows are much more formal in nature and best entered after you have gained some experience by participating in several match events. Championship shows are sponsored by various all-breed kennel clubs or in some instances by a club specializing in one particular breed of dog. The American Kennel

Club can provide you with the name of the all-breed kennel club in your area, and the Bichon Frise Club of America can let you know if there is a club in your vicinity. Refer to the "Useful Addresses and Literature" section at the end of this book.

How a Champion Is Made

For a dog registered with the AKC to become a champion, it must be awarded a total of fifteen championship points. These points are awarded to the best male and best female non-champions in each breed. The number of championship points that can be won at a particular show is based upon the number of entries in a dog's own breed and sex entered at the show. Of the fifteen points required, two of the wins must be what are called *majors* (i.e., three or more points). These two majors must be won under two different judges.

Catalogs sold at all championship shows list the particulars relevant to every dog entered. The catalog also lists the number of dogs required in each breed to win one through five points. Because the number of dogs necessary for the various number of points differs geographically, it is important to check the catalog at each show at which your male or female has been awarded points.

How to Enter a Championship Show

All show-giving clubs must issue what is called a *premium list*. A premium list contains all the information you will need to enter that club's show. A professional show superintendent or show secretary sends out these premium

---

TIP

Handling Classes

Many all-breed clubs sponsor handling classes for people who wish to show their own dogs. Professional dog handlers who will be able to offer you worthwhile tips both on handling in general and showing your Bichon specifically usually teach these classes.

In these classes you will learn a great deal about general ring procedures. At the same time your Bichon will become accustomed to being handled by strangers. As you attend more and more classes, you will observe your Bichon growing confident and less distracted. This makes good presentation easier for both you and your dog.

---

lists several weeks in advance of the closing date for entries.

You must advise the show superintendent in your area that you wish to receive all premium lists for shows in your area. A list of show superintendents can be obtained from the American Kennel Club. Once your name is entered on a show superintendent's list, you will continue to receive premium lists for all shows staged by that organization as long as you continue to show your dog.

The premium list will give you the date, location, and closing date for entries for a particular show. It will also list the entry fee, the judges for each of the breeds eligible to compete at the show, and the prizes that will be awarded in each breed.

CHECKLIST

Dog Show Classes

Listed are the classes in which you may enter your Bichon at American Kennel Club championship shows. Read the information contained in the premium list carefully. Often there are lower rates for puppy classes as well as other exceptions that you should be aware of. Each of the following classes is divided by sex, and all entries must be six months or older on the day of the show to be eligible.

Puppy Class: for entries under 12 months of age on the day of the show that are not champions.

12-to-18-Month Class: for entries at least 12 months but under 18 months of age on the day of the show that are not champions.

Novice Class: entries born in the United States, Canada, Mexico, or Bermuda that have not, before the closing date of entries, earned three first-place ribbons in the novice class or a first-place ribbon in bred-by-exhibitor, American-bred, or open class. Entries in this class may not have won any points toward their championships.

Bred-by-Exhibitor Class: for dogs except champions, six months of age and over, that are currently owned and exhibited by the same person or kennel who are the recognized breeders on the American Kennel Club records.

American-Bred Class: any nonchampion entry whelped in the United States as the result of a mating that took place in the United States.

Open Class: any entry, American or foreign bred, six months and older.

Usually the most experienced and mature show dogs are entered in the American-Bred and Open classes.

Also included in the premium list is the entry form that you will need to complete to enter the show. All the information you need to complete the entry form appears on your dog's AKC registration certificate. The information that you enter on this form will appear in the catalog on the day of the show.

Classes of Competition

It is important to note that in dog show terminology males are referred to as *dogs* and females as *bitches*. It is important to include the sex on the entry blank so that your Bichon is not put into the incorrect class. It is also important to remember that while at the show, only the males are dogs and your cherished female will be referred to as a bitch. Your entry will be called to the ring in that manner, so you must become accustomed to it.

As you read the requirements for the various dog show classes, it will become apparent that they are organized with respect to an entry's age and prior accomplishments. If you are a beginner, we strongly advise entering your Bichon in the puppy class if it is eligible. If your Bichon is over 12 months of age, enter it in

Puppy matches are an ideal place for the novice owner to learn how dog shows are run and to practice handling techniques.

the 12-to-18-month class. Those Bichons that will have passed the 18-month cutoff can be entered in the novice class. Judges are far more forgiving of immaturity and lack of experience in these classes than they are in some of the other classes that normally accommodate more seasoned dogs and handlers.

Professional Handlers

Professional handlers offer their services to those who do not wish to handle their own dogs at shows or who are unable to do so. These professionals can be contacted at most dog shows. When they have completed their work for the day, they are happy to discuss the possibility and practicality of having your Bichon professionally handled.

Handling Your Own Bichon

The foregoing explains the kinds of shows you may enter and how to go about doing so. Your preparation for entering shows must begin long before you actually exhibit at championship shows.

The beginner will have a great deal to learn. Much of what has to be learned is in books and magazine articles. Read everything that you can. Attend dog shows and observe the people in the ring with their Bichons. You will quickly see how much skilled handling enhances the dog's looks and its chances of winning.

The next step is to begin to master the art of handling your own Bichon. This can begin just as soon as you bring your puppy home. Teaching your puppy to stand still on the grooming

table while it is being brushed and combed is the initial phase of teaching it the proper stance in the show ring.

The judge examines the Bichon while the dog is posed on a table. This table is much like your grooming table at home; therefore it should not present a problem for your Bichon. It is important that your Bichon not be apprehensive when the judge attempts to examine it. You can practice staging this at home whenever strangers stop by.

Although showing is an enjoyable hobby, it takes hard work and a lot of study to master the art of handling your dog well. Patience and practice will help make you proficient. You will not become expert overnight.

Obedience trials: Obedience trials are held at both championship shows and matches, as

Obedience Trials give owner and dog an opportunity to show off their ability to learn and perform a series of set commands.

are the conformation events. The same informal entry procedures that apply to conformation matches apply here as well. The championship or "sanctioned" obedience trials are normally held in conjunction with conformation events and require entry ahead of time. They are handled in a more formal manner.

Obedience classes are definitely prerequisites here, because competition is highly precise and based entirely upon your dog's performing a set series of exercises. The exercises required in the various classes of competition range from basics such as heel, sit, and lie down in the novice class on through the sophisticated exercises of the utility and tracking dog levels that require scent discrimination and directed jumping.

Each level has a degree that can be earned after attaining qualifying scores at a given number of shows. The competition levels and corresponding degrees are as follows: Novice, which earns a Companion Dog degree (CD); Open, which earns the Companion Dog Excellent degree (CDX); and Utility, which earns the Utility Dog and Utility Dog Excellent degrees (UD and UDX). Tracking events earn the rare Tracking Dog and Tracking Dog Excellent titles (TD and TDX).

Undoubtedly because of their heritage as trick and circus dogs, Bichons have proven to be excellent candidates for obedience titles. Many have achieved their Companion Dog and Companion Dog Excellent degrees through the years, and the breed is proud to claim titleholders in even the most demanding of categories.

Agility: Agility competition is for all intents and purposes an obstacle course for dogs. Everyone involved (and everyone who watches) appears to be having the time of their lives. There are tunnels, catwalks, seesaws, and numerous other obstacles that the canine contestants must master off leash while being timed. Still in the early stages of growth, this event is catching on rapidly and will undoubtedly become one of the biggest attractions at all-breed dog shows.

Noncompetitive Pursuits

Canine Good Citizen test: Though this event does not achieve any AKC title, it is nonetheless an extremely valuable accomplishment. The purpose of the test is to demonstrate that the canine entered is well mannered and an asset to the community. There are ten parts to the test, and the dog must pass all ten to be awarded a certificate.

Therapy Dogs

Bichons have also proven themselves admirably as therapy dogs. This is a field in which dogs are trained to assist the sick, those with disabilities, and the aged. Because Bichons have a long history as companions and are of an easy-to-handle size, they are particularly suited to this work.

Bichons can be trained in a wide range of assistance roles. Their keen vision and hearing make them ideal companions for the hard-of-hearing and the sight impaired, warning their owners of situations or sounds that they might otherwise be incapable of recognizing.

An organization called Therapy Dogs International registers dogs that are temperamentally

The Bichon's wonderful temperament make the breed ideally suited to become Therapy Dogs. These happy little dogs visit hospitals, orphanages, and senior citizen homes throughout the country bringing a bit of sunshine into lives that might otherwise lack entertainment.

suitable for visiting hospitals and nursing homes. It has been found that there is great therapeutic value to the patients who come in contact with these dogs. Medical journals have substantiated stress reduction and lowered blood pressure as a result of these human-to-animal associations. Bichons, being the clowns that they are, add an element of humor and entertainment to the comfort they bring.

The Bichon Frise Club of America, the American Kennel Club, or your local obedience club can provide you with information about Therapy Dogs International.

Kennel Clubs

American Kennel Club
51 Madison Avenue
New York, NY 10010
Tel. (212) 696-8200
All Registration Information:
American Kennel Club
5580 Centerview Drive
Raleigh, NC 27606
Tel. (919) 233-9767
Web site: *www.akc.org*

Australian National Kennel Council
Royal Showgrounds
Ascot Vale 3032
Victoria, Australia
Web site: *www.ankc.aust.com*

Bichon Frise Club of America
Joanne Styles, Corresponding Secretary
186 Ash St. N.
Twin Falls, ID 83301
Web site: *www.bichon.org*

Canadian Kennel Club
89 Skyway Avenue, Unit 100
Etobicoke, Ontario M9W 6R4 Canada
Tel. (416) 675-5511
Web site: *www.ckc.ca/info*

The Kennel Club
1-5 Clargis Street
Piccadilly, London W1Y 8AB England
Web site: *www.the-kennel-club.org.uk*

United Kennel Club
100 E. Kilgore Road
Kalamazoo, MI 49001-5598
Web site: *www.ukcdogs.com*

Periodicals

The Bichon Frise Reporter
P.O. Box 6369
San Luis Obispo, CA 93412
Web site: *www.fix.net/~dogmag/bichon/*
    bichon-home.html

Dog Fancy
P.O. Box 6050
Mission Viejo, CA 92690-6050
Tel. (949) 855-8822
Web site: *www.dogfancy.com/dogfancy*

Dog World
P.O. Box 6050
Mission Viejo, CA 92690
Tel. (949) 855-8822
Web site: *www.dogworldmag.com*

*The Bichon is an amiable fellow and
many households find having two (or three!)
of these little white wonders is just that
much more fun.*

Dogs In Canada
Apex Publishers
89 Skyway Ave. #200
Etobicoke, Ontario., Canada M9W-6R4
Tel. (949) 855-8822
Web site: *www.dogsincanada.com/*

Dogs In Review
P.O. Box 6050
Mission Viejo, CA 92690
Tel. (949) 855-8822
Web site: *www.dogsinreview.com*

AKC Gazette
51 Madison Avenue
New York, NY 10010
Web site: *www.akc.org/pubs/index.cfm*

Books

Beauchamp, Richard G. *The Truth About Bichons*. Midway City, CA: Premiere Publications, Inc., 1998.
____. *The Simple Guide to Showing Your Dog*. Neptune City, NJ: TFH Publications, Inc., 2003.
Colflesh, Linda. *Making Friends (Training Your Dog Positively)*. New York: Howell Book House, 1990.
Ransom, E. Jackie. *The Bichon Frise*. London: H. F. & G. Witherby, Ltd., 1990.
Stubbs, Barbara. *The Complete Bichon Frise*. New York: Howell Book House, 1990.
Squire, Dr. Ann. *Understanding Man's Best Friend*. New York: Macmillan Publishing Company, 1991.

Pet Travel Publications

"Traveling with Your Pet: the AAA Petbook"
The Automobile Association of America (AAA)
Tel. (800) 222-4357

"Vacationing with Your Pet Guide"
Pet Friendly Publications
2327 Ward Road
Pocomoke City, MD 28851

Poison Control

National ASPCA Animal Poison Control Center
Tel (888) 426-4435

Therapy Dog Organizations

Therapy Dogs International, Inc.
88 Bartley Road
Flanders, NJ 07836
Tel. (973) 252-9800
Web site: *www.tdi-dog.org*

Taking advantage of the many services offered by purebred dog organizations will make life with your Bichon mutually beneficial.

94 **I N D E X**

About the Author

Richard G. (Rick) Beauchamp has been involved with the Bichon Frise breed since its earliest days in America. He has bred more than 70 champions in the breed, among them many Best in Show and Variety Group winners. He owned Ch. Chaminade Mr. Beau Monde, the top-producing sire in the breed (65 champions) and was breeder of Ch. Beau Monde the Fire Cracker, top-producing dam in the breed (17 champions). He participated in writing the American Kennel Club standard for the breed. Rick is an AKC judge and judges purebred dogs in every major country of the world, along with lecturing and writing about dogs of all breeds. He judged Bichon Frises at the 2004 Crufts show in England, the world's largest dog show.

Acknowledgments

The author is indebted to the breed's pioneers but even more so to today's breeders, who carry the breed on to even greater accomplishments and respect. A very special thanks also goes to Marcy Rosenbaum, whose support and encouragement through a rough patch in the road allowed me to complete the revision of this book.

Important Note

This pet owner's guide tells the reader how to buy and care for a Bichon Frise. The author and the publisher consider it important to point out that the advice given in the book primarily concerns normally developed puppies from a good breeder—that is, dogs of excellent physical health and good character.

Anyone who adopts a fully grown dog should be aware that the animal has already formed its basic impressions of human beings. The new owner should watch the animal carefully, including its behavior toward humans, and should meet the previous owner. If the dog comes from a shelter, it may be possible to get some information on the dog's background and peculiarities there. Some dogs, as a result of bad experiences with humans, behave in an unnatural manner or may even bite. Only people that have experience with dogs should take in such animals.

Caution is further advised in the association of children with dogs, in meeting with other dogs, and in exercising the dog without a leash.

Even well-behaved and carefully supervised dogs sometimes do damage to someone else's property or cause accidents. It is therefore in the owner's interest to be adequately insured against such eventualities, and we strongly urge all dog owners to purchase a liability policy that covers their dog.

Cover Photos

Front cover and inside front cover: Isabelle Francais; back cover and inside back cover: Pets by Paulette.

Photo Credits

John Ashbey: page 84; Norvia Behling: pages 23, 35 (top right); Kent Dannen: pages 14, 21, 28, 29 (top right), 30 (top right), 31 (bottom right), 40 (top left), 45, 50, 51, 56, 82, 85, 86, 90, 93; Isabelle Francais: pages 8, 20, 22, 27, 29 (bottom right), 30 (top left), 32, 33, 36, 37, 40 (bottom left), 44, 46 (top and bottom left), 47, 48, 59, 60, 64, 65, 66, 76 (top left and right), 77, 80; Gressick: pages 58, 61; Pets by Paulette: pages 2, 3, 4, 5, 7, 9, 15, 16, 18, 24, 25, 31 (top right), 35 (top and bottom right), 41, 49 (top and bottom right), 54, 55, 57, 63, 67, 68, 72, 73, 74, 75, 78, 81, 91, 92; The Standard Image: page 11; Connie Summers: pages 19, 69, 89.

© Copyright 2006 by Barron's Educational Series, Inc.

All inquiries should be addressed to:
Barron's Educational Series, Inc.
250 Wireless Boulevard
Hauppauge, NY 11788
www.barronseduc.com

ISBN-13: 978-0-7641-3405-0
ISBN-10: 0-7641-3405-1

Library of Congress Catalog Card No. 2006042774

Library of Congress Cataloging-in-Publication Data
Beauchamp, Richard G.
  Bichon frise : everything about purchase, care, nutrition, breeding, behavior, and training / Richard G. Beauchamp.—2nd ed.
    p. cm. — (A Complete pet owner's manual)
  Includes bibliographical references and index.
  ISBN-13: 978-0-7641-3405-0
  ISBN-10: 0-7641-3405-1
  1. Bichon frise. I. Beauchamp, Richard G. Bichons frise. II. Title. III. Series.

SF429.B52B43 2006
636.72—dc22   2006042774

Printed in China
9 8 7 6 5 4 3 2 1